SOCCER
TECHNIQUES IN
PICTURES

Michael Brown

Book Consultant: Tony Johnson,
former professional soccer player,
American Soccer League, United Soccer League

A Perigee Book

Perigee Books are published by
The Putnam Publishing Group
200 Madison Avenue
New York, NY 10016

Cover design by Lisa Amoroso

Library of Congress Cataloging-in-Publication Data

Brown, Michael, date.
    Soccer techniques in pictures / Michael Brown: book consultant, Tony Johnson.
        p.   cm.
    Summary: Text and photographs introduce the fundamental skills of soccer, the most
popular sport in the world.
    ISBN 0-399-51701-4
    1. Soccer—Pictorial works—Juvenile literature. [1. Soccer.]
I. Title.
GV943.25.B76 1991   91-18302 CIP AC
796.334'2'0222—dc20

Front cover photograph
© by Brian Drake/SportsChrome East-West

Printed in the United States of America
    3 4 5 6 7 8 9 10

CONTENTS

Introduction

Soccer enthusiasts of all levels are sure to profit from this handy how-to guide to developing superior soccer techniques. While tactics, rules, coaching strategies, and the development of strength, stamina, and flexibility are all important to soccer, all these must be built on a foundation of sound technique. Using step-by-step illustrations, this book will take a close look at

- ball control;
- kicking or striking the ball;
- heading;
- dribbling;
- tackling;
- the throw-in and other special techniques;
- goalkeeping;
- elementary tactics.

With the exception of the special skills that must be developed by goalkeepers, all the above techniques are absolutely necessary in order for players of all offensive and defensive positions to master control of the ball and consequently to fully enjoy and play the game well.

Soccer is beyond dispute the most popular sport in the world. In the United States, more youngsters and adults are now playing the game than ever before. A sport that's played by 15 million people in the U.S. and more than 50 million players on six continents must have a lot to recommend it.

Soccer's basic premises are shared by many sports: maneuver a ball into a goal, and stop your opponent from doing the same. However, in soccer there are a variety of demanding techniques that must be learned before even a pickup game can be played. These techniques are made all the more demanding by the subtle tactics, team strategy, psychology, and stamina required. Combined with a complex rhythm—the ball responds almost imperceptibly to the feather-light stroke of a foot one moment, then slams into the goal at 90 miles an hour the next—it is both the ultimate team game and a sport with high appeal for the individual.

A game that can be successfully played at all levels by children and adults of all heights, sizes, and builds, soccer is not only a safe sport, it's one that develops stamina, overall strength, flexibility, quick thinking, and resourcefulness better than any I know.

One technique that is unique to soccer is that of controlling or trapping the ball with the feet or body. This skill is so important to good play that it is the first technique described in this book. From there we move on, building upon previously learned skills to develop new techniques. While you read this book and improve your soccer skills, keep these four points in mind:

- To be a good player, you must master the techniques on *both your left and right sides.* It doesn't matter what your dominant side is, right or left, all soccer players must use their right and left feet and legs with equal ease. Throughout this book, your two legs are referred to as your support leg, on which you carry your weight while manipulating the ball, and your *kicking* leg, with which you manipulate the ball.

Generally speaking, it is common practice to play a ball moving across your body from right to left with your left foot, and a ball moving across your body from left to right with your right foot. That is only a general rule, however. The situation you find yourself in will determine which foot you choose.

Practice is essential.

- A soccer game does not provide enough access to the ball to develop good techniques; therefore, *practice sessions are essential.* Without practice, which you should take slowly at first, then "at speed" and under pressure, the techniques won't be readily available to you when game time comes.
- Practice only when you're feeling physically and mentally alert, and try to make your practice fun. If you practice until you are too tired to perform the techniques correctly, you'll end up practicing bad habits that will resurface in the game.
- Frequently, when describing the techniques in this book, I tell you to move into the line of flight of the ball. This is always good advice, because when you do this you can avoid having to reach out unnecessarily far with your leg or having to head the ball while off-balance. Keeping good balance gives you your chance to execute the techniques properly.

Let's face it, a game of real soccer doesn't always give you the chance to use the techniques exactly as they are described here. Often, you're lucky to touch the ball at all. Nevertheless, you must remember to move to the ball the best you can even if you can't line up directly in the line of flight. Then you've got to choose the technique that you think will give you the best chance of success, whether you're off-balance or not. And you have to do all this in a split second.

Discover what the pros have learned. During their careers, these players have spent hours just standing around the field in small groups, juggling the ball with various parts of their body, chatting, and working the ball among themselves, oblivious of the time. Like the pros, you'll discover that skill work is fun work.

Juggling the ball.

1 Ball Control

Before learning to play a ball sport, the players must learn to control the ball. This is the most basic and important skill; in soccer, the rest of your game cannot fully develop until you have learned to "trap" a ball, and when good soccer is being played, ball-control skills are equally important in defense and attack.

Specifically, ball control is the ability to absorb the force of or cushion a moving ball, whether in the air or bouncing or rolling on the ground. Real ball control leaves the player free to shoot, dribble, or pass at will. The ball may be "trapped" with any part of the body except hands or arms: feet, thighs, chest, or head.

In developing this skill, a few basic principles are universally true:

- You cannot control the ball if you cannot control your body. In the course of a game, you will start, stop, change pace, change direction, run sideways, backward, and jump, all in reaction to other players and the ball. Therefore, always maintain a poised position when you are anywhere near the action. This means keeping your weight forward on the balls of the feet, your knees slightly bent, feet shoulder width apart, arms out for balance, and head up. Of course, you must look at the ball and concentrate on it as you are trapping it. However, good players minimize the time they concentrate on the ball at their feet so they can maximize the time they spend scanning the field for opportunities.
- In most situations, you should get as much of your body in line with the flight of the ball as possible. That way, if you don't manage to cushion the ball as softly as you'd like, it will be blocked by some part of your body and stay more or less near where you are.
- Always take a relaxed stance as you keep your eyes on the ball, judging its flight. Imagine as you decide which type of trap to use that you are about to gently catch something soft and breakable.
- At the moment of contact with the ball, the body part you are using to trap the ball should relax and "give" a little, absorbing the force of the ball, further slowing it, and helping to put it completely under your control.

It's good practice to cultivate the ability to be creative with the ball on your second touch. As your game develops, you'll find that your opponents give you little or no time to control the ball and decide what to do next. It's not easy to concentrate with them breathing down your neck, but relaxed concentration (and practice) is the absolute key to successful ball control under pressure. When you do master the skill of second-touch control, it will be a source of great satisfaction to you and a delight for onlookers to watch.

A sole trap.

Trapping with the Feet

TRAPPING WITH THE SOLE OF THE FOOT

Various parts of the foot are used to trap the ball, depending on the situation and what the player hopes to do next. Trapping with the sole of the foot is probably the easiest method; you'll use it most frequently on a ball that drops to the ground directly in front of you. Its major drawback is that it usually takes a long time to develop a productive second touch of the ball.

Assume a position with your weight on your supporting (nontrapping) leg, which should be slightly bent at the knee. Your trapping foot should be poised on its toes ready to move up and over the ball. As the ball approaches, raise your trapping leg from the hip, keeping the knee slightly bent and relaxed.

Make contact with the ball with the sole of your foot, just as the ball lands on the ground. Make sure to keep your ankle relaxed.

TRAPPING WITH THE INSIDE OF THE FOOT

The inside of the foot from heel to big toe is the longest area of the foot and the most reliable part with which to control the ball. The inside-of-the-foot trap is the most frequently used trap and is particularly good for controlling a ball rolling along the ground.

Poise yourself across the line of the approaching ball. Lean in the direction of the ball and turn slightly in the direction of the trapping leg. The trapping leg with knee slightly bent is turned at the hips, so the foot is at a 90-degree angle to the ball. As the ball arrives, the trapping leg is drawn up, forming a slight angle with the inside of the foot and the ground—a wedge into which the ball will fit.

The leg, ankle, and foot are all relaxed and, as contact is made with the ball, pulled back slightly to absorb the impact of the ball.

Using the foot to reach for the ball.

Withdrawing the foot to absorb the impact of the ball.

TRAPPING WITH THE OUTSIDE OF THE FOOT

Trapping the ball with the outside of your foot is a good way to quickly set the ball up for your next move. This trap can also create some confusion in the mind of the defender, who won't easily be able to foresee in which direction you intend to move.

From a poised position, as the ball nears, stretch the trapping leg toward it with your foot turned out and toe pointed down. As the ball arrives, the trapping leg moves across the center line of your body, then your relaxed trapping foot makes contact with a sweeping motion down and across the ball.

Using your feet to trap balls in the air is done exactly the same way as you trap balls on the ground. Always remember to follow the basic trapping principles outlined above. Whether or not to use the foot or some other part of the body to control a ball in the air will depend on your assessment of the overall situation. The objective, however, will nearly always be the same: to drop the ball immediately to your feet so that you may do something creative with it.

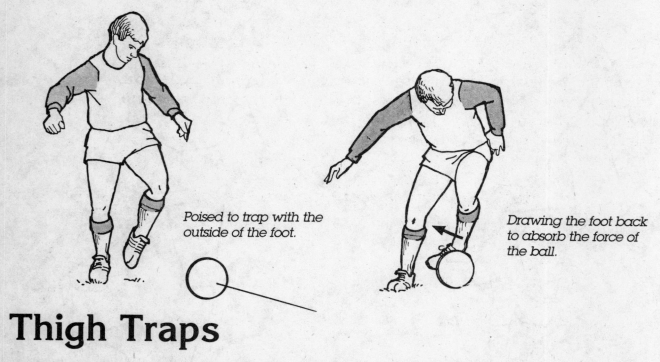

Poised to trap with the outside of the foot.

Drawing the foot back to absorb the force of the ball.

Thigh Traps

Thigh traps are used to control balls that are dropping from above or moving parallel to the ground.

For balls moving parallel to the ground, the side of the thigh is used. From a poised position, across the line of flight of the ball, turn the body slightly sideways to the ball in the direction of the trapping leg. Raise your thigh at a right angle to the body, with the inside of the thigh to be used as the trapping surface and the lower leg relaxed at a 90-degree angle to the thigh. As the ball arrives, relax and withdraw the thigh backward, allowing the ball to drop gently from the thigh to your most effective tools, your feet.

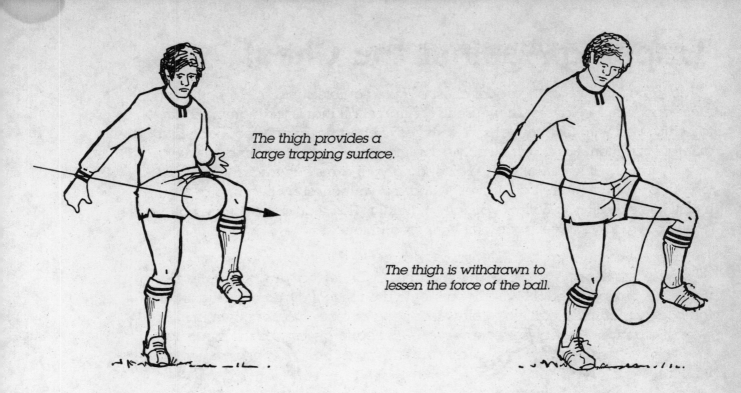

The thigh provides a large trapping surface.

The thigh is withdrawn to lessen the force of the ball.

The top of the thigh can be used to control a ball dropping from above. Facing the ball across its line of flight and in a poised position, raise the thigh directly in front of the body at a 90-degree angle to the flight of the ball, keeping the lower leg relaxed. As the ball arrives at your thigh, give in to it, withdraw backward, and allow it to drop gently to the ground. This is more difficult than it looks due to the tenseness and roundness of the thigh muscle when the thigh is raised, but very useful when perfected.

Any part of the body except hands or arms may be used to trap the ball.

The principles of basic trapping remain the same.

Trapping Against the Chest

The large flat area of the upper chest is a predictable surface that both male and female players safely use to control a ball that is too high in the air to be trapped with feet or thighs. Two types of chest traps are used, each in a different situation. For a ball quickly traveling parallel to the ground, first step directly into the line of flight while extending your arms outward and forward to your body. When the ball arrives, withdraw your chest by bending at the hips while exhaling to hollow your chest slightly. This should deflect the ball gently down to your feet, ready for your second touch.

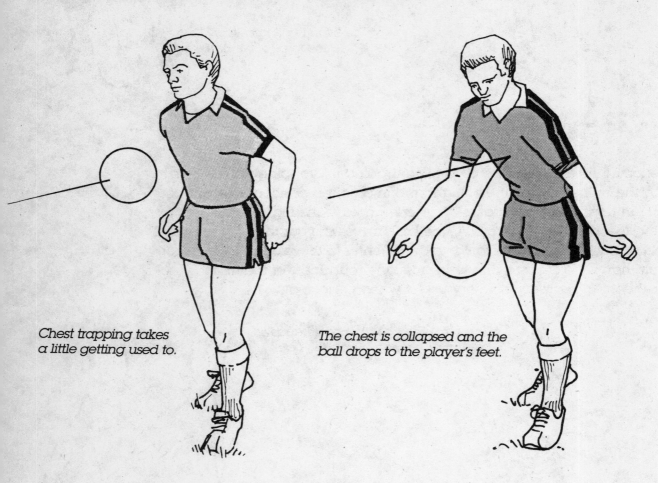

Chest trapping takes a little getting used to.

The chest is collapsed and the ball drops to the player's feet.

The second method of chest trapping is used for balls dropping from above. Move across the line of flight of the ball, arms out, not forward as in the previous trap, but held slightly back instead, forcing the chest forward and up. As the ball arrives, lean back farther, with your chin tucked in, forming a "table" of your chest and bending your knees to absorb the impact of the ball.

After resting on your chest, the ball should roll down the front of your body and drop, ready to use, at your feet.

Using the techniques just described should help you develop good ball control. Don't think of developing ball control as an odious chore that must be completed before the real fun can start—good players are the ones who spend many afternoons just hanging out at the field with a few buddies, juggling and manipulating the ball for pure pleasure. They know ball control is an enjoyment worth developing for its own sake.

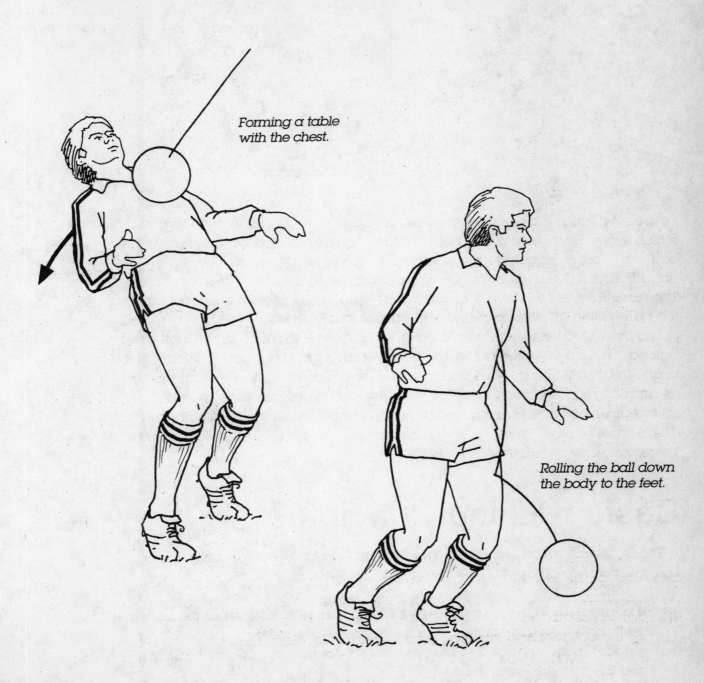

Forming a table with the chest.

Rolling the ball down the body to the feet.

2 Kicking or Striking the Ball

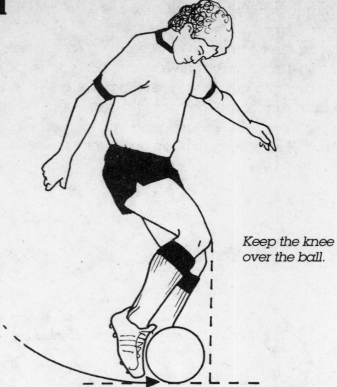

Keep the knee over the ball.

Passing, which is the essence of the team aspect of soccer, and shooting, which scores goals and is the "point" of the game, both depend on kicking the ball well. This essential, frequently used skill must be perfected ambidextrously, using both your left and right feet on still and moving balls. Successful players work very hard at developing sound techniques for striking the ball well in all situations and with all parts of both feet.

The first objective in learning kicking techniques is to make sure that the ball goes exactly where you want it to go—not just in a general direction, but to an *exact destination*. Until you can do this, it is pointless to try to hit the ball as hard as you can into the goal or sixty-five yards downfield. Remember, your teammates need passes that they can control quickly and easily, and it doesn't matter how forceful a shot is if it isn't heading toward the goal mouth. Therefore, easy does it to start with.

Basic Kicking Principles

Regardless of which of the many kicking techniques you are using, certain basic principles will apply:

- The large, flat parts of the foot—the instep, the inside (from big toe to heel), and the outside (from little toe to heel)—are the three best kicking surfaces. Both the toes and the heel are too round for accurate kicking, and the toes are easily injured.

- The power in a kick comes from a full swing of the kicking leg and the rate of speed with which your foot strikes the ball. Balls on the ground should be struck when your foot is at its lowest point and the knee of your kicking foot is directly above the ball.
- The follow through of your kicking foot should be along the intended flight-line of the ball.

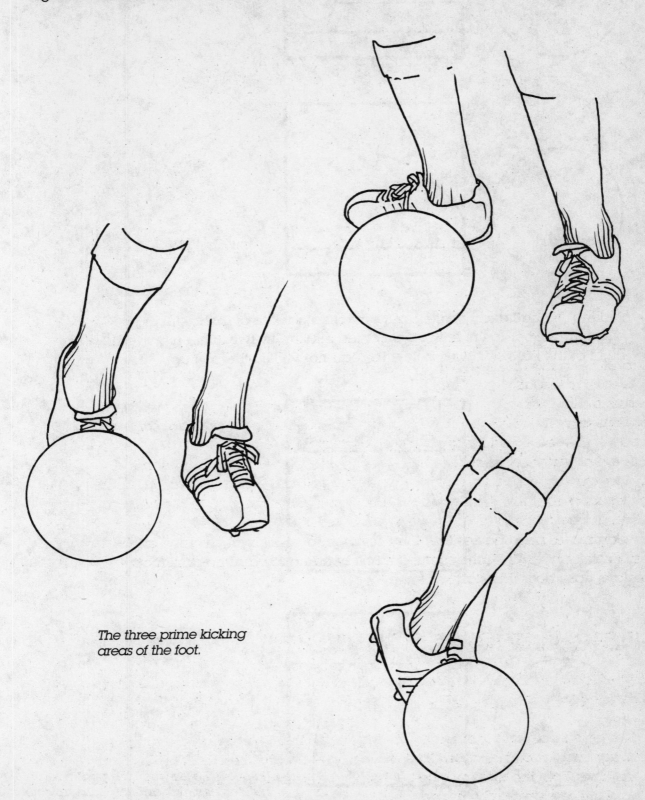

The three prime kicking areas of the foot.

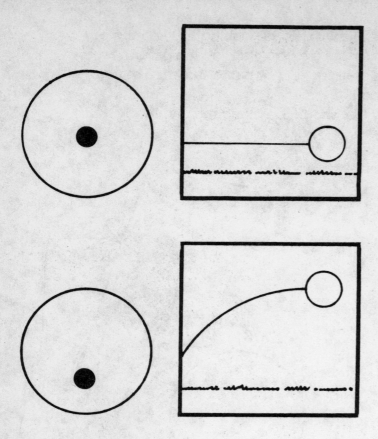

- Striking the ball dead center results in a straight line of flight; striking it off-center, either to the left or right of the midline, will result in a curved flight of the ball; striking it below the equator will lift the ball up.

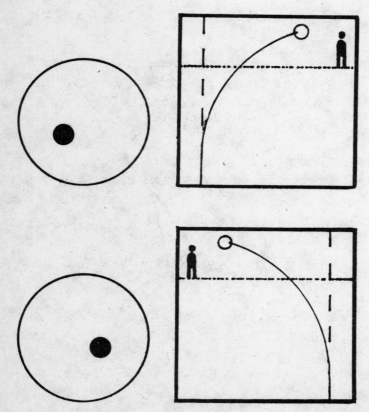

Relationship between the position on the ball that is struck and the ball's trajectory.

Inside-of-the-Foot Kick

The foot is turned outward as it is drawn back.

Lining everything up.

The inside-of-the-foot kick is the most frequently used kick in soccer, particularly for passing. That's because it is the most accurate. Luckily, it is also the easiest kick to master. In learning this skill, it is helpful to think of the action as pushing rather than kicking the ball. Then, as you develop this technique, you add power to the stroke.

From a poised position, step with the nonkicking foot directly along the intended line of the pass. Plant the nonkicking support foot alongside the ball, just far enough away to allow free swinging of the kicking leg. Your support foot should be pointing in the direction you wish the ball to travel. Your weight will be directly above the ball as your kicking foot moves forward, ankle locked at a 90-degree angle to the intended flight-line of the ball.

During the kick, the foot moves forward low to the ground and makes contact with the center of the ball. Your kicking foot then follows through along the ball's intended line of travel. After spotting the target, it's important to remember to keep your head down over the ball and concentrate. If you let your head pop up, your pass will pop up too. Your pass will then be inaccurate and easy to intercept.

Instep Drive

The instep drive is the heavy artillery of kicks. It is most frequently used for goal kicks, free kicks, long passes such as crosses, and defensive clearances.

In a poised position, step toward the ball from an angle of about 30 degrees from the intended flight-line. For a powerful shot, take a longish last stride as you plant your nonkicking support foot alongside the ball, pointing in the direction you want the ball to go. The way you plant your nonkicking foot is very important. It should be far enough away from the ball to allow your kicking leg to swing freely. Avoid planting your support foot much ahead of the ball—this can easily result in an injury to your kicking foot, since it is

A cocked kicking leg with a firm plant alongside the ball.

Contact at the center of the ball.

18

destined to swing into the ground. (The only exception to this is in a case where you're kicking a ball rolling rapidly away from you.)

Just before you strike the ball, straighten your leg firmly and forcefully. This adds power to your shot. In striking the ball, the ankle of your kicking foot should be locked and your toes pointing down.

Hit the ball right in its center with the laces of your soccer shoe. Remember to keep your head down and to concentrate on the ball. Following through with your kicking foot along the intended line of flight of the ball will help you develop power and accuracy.

A strong follow through.

If you want the ball to travel upward, keep your support foot alongside the ball but also slightly back. Strike the ball as you normally would for an instep drive, but make contact slightly below its equator. Many players, especially those with large feet, might need to turn the kicking foot a few degrees to the outside of their body in order to make good contact with their laces.

Again, remember to follow through with the kicking foot moving along the intended line of flight of the ball, keeping your head down as you do so. Don't let the follow through cross over the midline of your body.

The head stays low throughout upward motion of the follow through.

The support foot is planted
well behind the ball.

The body is leaning back and contact
is slightly underneath the ball.

Outside-of-the-Foot Kick

The outside of the foot is used to direct the ball to your right or left quickly, without the weight shift that other kicks need. It's not a particularly powerful kick, but it can be the most deceptive kick in your arsenal. Although this is a *kicking* technique, many players try to simply flick the ball with their foot only; the limp ankle required to do this means a serious loss of control.

Here's a better method: From a poised position, plant your nonkicking support foot well to the side of and behind the ball. The toes of your supporting foot should be pointed approximately 30 degrees away from the intended flight of the ball.

As you kick, the toes of your kicking foot are pointed down and turned slightly inward as your leg and foot move forward and out in the direction of the intended flight of the ball. Your foot remains pointed down and in during the follow through. The area just to the outside of your shoelaces, from behind the little toe to the ankle, should make contact with the center of the ball. There should be a relatively short follow through in the direction of the intended flight of the ball; keep your head down as you complete the follow through.

The support foot at an angle to the intended line of flight.

Firm contact with a locked ankle.

A short follow through.

Chip Shot

Chip shots get the ball to rise very quickly and, after lofting over the helpless defense players, drop gently behind them. It's a wonderfully effective shot, but not one to use for power or distance. Anyone can easily master this technique on balls that are rolling toward them; it is manageable and very useful on a dead ball, but it's quite difficult to do while running with the ball.

To chip the ball, approach it from a slight angle. Plant your nonkicking foot a little closer than you normally would for most other kicks. As you plant your support foot, draw the lower leg of your kicking foot back from the knee, flexing the knee as much as is reasonably possible. Then snap it quickly forward, moving your foot through the center of the ball well below its equator. You may want to point your toes down as you did for the instep drive. Or, try turning your foot sideways, making contact with the ball inside your shoelaces; this is more like the technique used in the side-of-the-foot pass. Experiment and see which one gives you the best results.

At contact, lean back and imagine you are scooping the ball over the defense. For short chips, there is little or no follow through. For a chip that must cover a longer distance, you'll want to follow through by raising the knee of your kicking foot. Check your technique by looking for backspin on a successful chip shot.

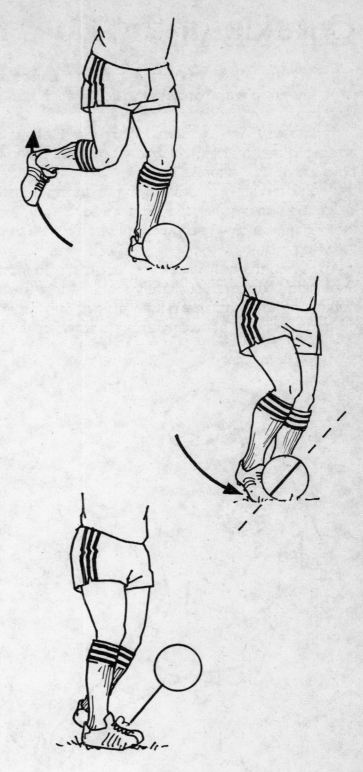

The kicking leg drawn sharply back.

Contact well underneath the ball.

Little or no follow through.

Curve Balls

If you have already begun to master the instep drive, it's time to begin experimenting with bending the ball, which can be done from left to right or vice versa.

It may seem like an intimidating and difficult skill to master, but in reality it is much easier to "bend" a soccer ball than it is to throw a curve with a baseball or slice a tennis ball.

It's a particularly useful technique during free kicks when you need to curve the ball around packed defenses. Curve balls are also useful to keep the ball inbounds when passing from midfield to a teammate breaking down the wing.

Approach the ball just as you would for an instep drive, but plant your nonkicking support foot slightly to the rear of the ball. You want to get the ball up in the air at least a little, since it will curve better in the air than on the ground. It's not particularly important *where* the toes of your nonkicking foot

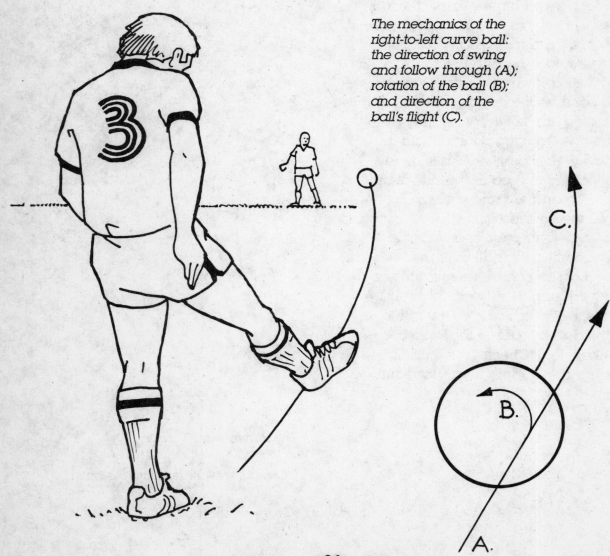

The mechanics of the right-to-left curve ball: the direction of swing and follow through (A); rotation of the ball (B); and direction of the ball's flight (C).

are pointed, since this will have little effect on the ball's direction. Strike the ball in the same fashion as you would for an instep drive, but off-center, keeping the toes of your kicking foot extended. Strike *across* the ball rather than through its center. If your kicking foot hits the outer third of the ball at just inside the laces of your boot, the ball will swerve across your body. If you stroke across the ball, striking the inner third of it with the outside of your bootlaces, it will bend out, away from you. The follow through should extend the natural direction of the stroke, either away from or across your body, and not follow the flight of the ball. Sidespin is what causes the ball to curve; check your technique by looking for sidespin. The ball will curve in the direction of the spin—a clockwise spin will give you a clockwise curve, and vice versa.

Give it a try. As a teammate said to me a few years ago, "Everything I hit seems to bend a little anyway; I might as well learn to use it!"

The mechanics of the left-to-right curve ball: the direction of swing and follow through (A); rotation of the ball (B); and direction of the ball's flight (C).

C.

B.

A.

Volleying the Ball

Normally, well-drilled soccer players prefer to settle the ball to the ground at their feet before trying to make their next move with it. However, when you're under pressure or must perform quickly, you may need to volley the ball while it's still on the fly, without trapping it first. There are a number of advanced and difficult volleying techniques. For example, the side volley is used for waist-high balls. Then there's the half volley for balls that are just about to drop to the ground, which is described in the goalkeeping section of this book. The overhead volley is used to kick balls that are over your head.

Two types of volleys are used more often than all the others combined, and fortunately, they are two of the easiest to execute. These are the instep volley, which is used for a quick, long defensive clearance from in front of your own goal; and the side-of-the-foot volley pass, which will give a teammate an accurate and controllable pass.

All volleys including these two "easy" volleys share the same basic principles as all the other kicks described previously. Both support and kicking feet are used in exactly the same way.

The side-of-the-foot volley pass is hit just like a side-of-the-foot pass. The instep volley is hit just like the instep drive. The only difference between these volleys and the ground passes is that your foot is making contact while the ball is still in the air.

Since you are trying to hit a moving ball with a moving foot, it is very hard to accurately select the spot on the ball you'll contact with your kick. Also, the ball will tend to fly all over the map when you first start practicing a volley. Because of this, you must observe some extra precautions when trying to volley

A side volley. Only highly experienced players have a good chance of success with this shot.

The overhead volley. This should only be attempted with the aid of a coach and never by an inexperienced player.

the ball. While the ball is coming toward you, try to still yourself so that you may, with a motionless head, judge the flight of the ball as accurately as possible.

In general, let the ball drop as low as possible before attempting your kick. The higher the ball, the more difficult it will be to hit.

As mentioned earlier, the ball is struck exactly the same as it would be for an instep drive or a side-of-the-foot pass. If you want the ball to go downward, then you must strike a little above its middle. If you want the ball to go up, you must strike the ball slightly below the middle.

For both types of volleys, your body will tend to lean back, and volleys have a marked tendency to fly higher than you would like, so concentrate hard on keeping your head down.

Side-of-the-foot volley pass.

The instep volley—a great tool for defensive clearances.

3 Heading

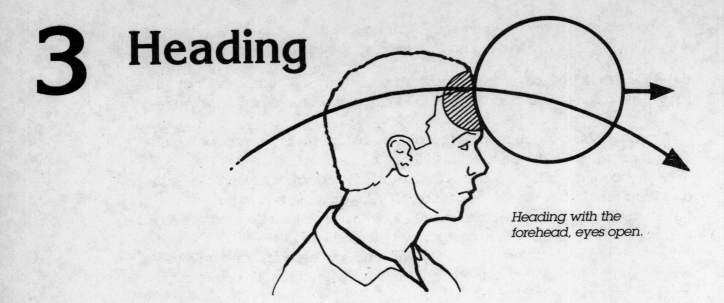

Heading with the forehead, eyes open.

Some coaches seem to think that if a perfect game of soccer were played, the ball would never leave the ground. Ground level is where the player's feet are, and that is where they are best able to control the ball. But in a real game in the real world, the ball spends a great deal of time in the air. For instance, if you wait to play the ball at your feet in a crowded penalty area right in front of the goal, you will certainly lose it before you have the chance to play it. This is the sort of situation where heading techniques are the most effective means to use.

Besides, soccer is supposed to be fun and entertaining. Can you imagine that "perfect" game without the electrifying moment when one player leaps, head and shoulders above the other players, to strike a perfectly placed header?

Basic Heading Principles

Heading is an indispensable skill for all players. Numerous types of headers can be used all over the field, in many different situations. There are head shots, high, wide defensive headers, direction-changing headers, flick headers, diving headers, and at the highest levels, even head traps. With all this variety, all good headers have a few basic principles in common:

- The eyes must be kept open when heading. You must continue to watch the ball as it makes contact with your head. It takes some practice to do this, since your natural reflexes tell you to duck and blink. However, keeping your eyes open will increase your accuracy tremendously and help to eliminate the risk of injury from "heading" with your nose.

- The area on your forehead between the eyebrows and the hairline is the surface that should be used to strike the ball. The skull bone is thickest here, so it's the least likely part of your head to be injured. It's also one of the flatter surfaces on your head. Always keep your tongue in your mouth and your mouth shut to avoid tongue and dental injuries.

- You must actively direct the ball, striking it with your head. Don't simply allow the ball to hit your head and rebound off it. Active control will not only increase your choice of direction of the ball, it will also help to lessen the risk injury.

For powerful heading, the feet, legs, torso, and neck must also be involved in the striking movement and follow through.

Heading on the Ground

It is easiest to head the ball while standing, although you can also successfully head while running. You must first carefully judge the flight of the ball and then move into a position to intercept it. Assume a wide, well-balanced stance, preferably with one foot in front of the other, since you will need to shift your body weight backward and then forward during the heading motion.

Make sure to keep your eyes open, following the flight of the ball as it approaches. Your arms should be held out to your sides for balance.

As the ball nears, lean back slightly, cocking your entire upper body from the waist, then snap forward, head, neck, and trunk driven by the legs and buttocks. Follow through with your upper body in the direction you want the header to go. The follow through will help you by adding power and accuracy to the header.

A follow through down toward a teammate's feet or the opponent's goal.

The whole body is coiled.

Hitting the ball rather than letting the ball hit you.

Heading in the Air

Once you've developed some ability to head while standing, you should begin to work on heading while jumping. Although the basics are similar, the stable power base of your legs is eliminated when you jump. You must also develop the ability to time your leap perfectly, heading the ball when you are at your highest point and well above the heads of the opponents who may surround you.

Judge the flight of the ball, then move quickly into its line of flight, using a one-footed takeoff to jump upward and at the same time thrust the nonjumping knee upward. This type of jump helps you leave the ground without breaking stride, thus converting horizontal running momentum into vertical leaping momentum. (A two-footed takeoff may also be called for at times—for instance, in a crowd where there is little room to develop more power.) Holding your arms out from your sides will help you to maintain balance while in the air and to develop power.

As the ball arrives and you are reaching the apex of your leap, you should have cocked your upper body slightly backward, pushing your hips forward. Strike the ball with your forehead, thrusting with head, neck, and torso while bending at the waist. In following through along the intended line of flight, your legs will naturally move forward, balancing your body.

*A one-footed takeoff
feels the most natural.*

*The body is coiled,
ready to strike.*

Heading from the waist.

Redirecting the Ball

To one degree or another all headers redirect the ball. The exact method of redirection will depend on what your desired result is. If you want to head downward at the goal or to a teammate's feet, you'll need to strike the ball above its equator. Your head must actually be slightly above the ball as you strike down on it. To head the ball up and over opponents and away from danger, you'll need to strike the ball slightly below its equator while your leap is still carrying you upward.

To redirect the ball to the left or right, bend your torso slightly and withdraw your head and upper body to the side of the line of flight of the ball as it approaches. As usual, your forehead remains the striking surface, and you strike and follow through in the intended direction of the ball.

The head is moved to the side of the line of flight.

The forehead is still the preferred striking surface.

Skim and Flick Headers

Slight, glancing headers are also useful at times. They are the only types of headers in which the ball strikes you instead of you striking the ball. Skim headers send high passes on in the same direction they were traveling, while flick headers slightly redirect a ball that is traveling parallel to the ground at head height. These headers should only be done with a ball that is going to land a glancing blow to your head, not a direct one. Let's say you're playing forward, near midfield, facing back toward your own goal as a teammate in defense has just hit a long clearance upfield. Lean back and allow the ball to skim off your forehead, continuing on into your opponents' half of the field. Very little extra body motion is necessary. An alert teammate can run on to the ball and be in front of your opponents' goal with no one to beat but the keeper.

Glancing headers off the forehead are also useful for slightly changing the direction of near postcorner kicks, redirecting them into the goal. The same principle as for skim headers applies, just allow the ball to glance off your forehead while giving your head a slight flick from the neck; very little body motion is needed.

A skim head.

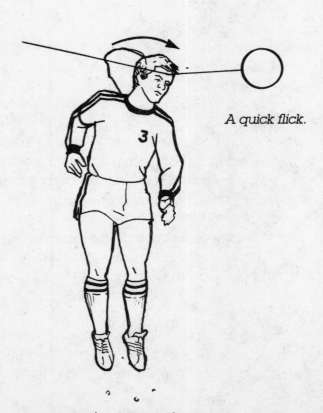

A quick flick.

4 Dribbling

Dribbling is the art of moving about the soccer field with the ball under your personal control. With gentle touches of the ball, you keep the ball at or close to your feet within playable distance. All players envy a really good dribbler and all players, both forwards and defenders, need to be able to dribble well.

Dribbling may be done in any direction—forward, backward, or across the field—at great speed or nearly at a standstill, straight ahead or with many changes of direction.

Some players, having once heard that soccer is a passing game, are too hesitant to dribble. This is unfortunate, since there are some times when dribbling is the best thing to do. When a quick dash with the ball will put you in front of your opponents' goal; when you must weave your way out of a crowd of players who are blocking all your passing opportunities; or when you must delay and hold on to the ball until your teammates can take better positions or help you out; these are all reasonable times to dribble.

Basic Principles

All good players develop their own style of dribbling. Regardless of individual differences, there are certain principles that all successful dribblers follow:

- Keep the ball within one stride of your feet so that you may change the ball's speed or direction quickly.
- Stay well-balanced so that you may change your speed or direction instantly. When running with the ball, stride as naturally as possible.
- Be able to maintain complete and constant control of the ball without looking down at it; keep it in your peripheral vision so you're free to look for opportunities and react to your opponent.
- In the course of a game, a good dribbler will avoid repetitive ploys and instead will bypass defenders using a variety of means. When you feint, hoping to throw the defender off-balance, it must be done in a wholehearted, convincing manner. This gives the opponent time to perceive, and then react to, the fake. Your opponent will be a lot faster without the ball than you are with it, so make him commit to a direction before you try to take off in another.

You can dribble with any part of your foot. Players use the inside, the outside, and the laces. They dribble with the sole and even the heel, and occasionally you'll even see a quick toe poke thrown in.

Let's look at some specific practical techniques to which you can add your own personal touch.

Running with the Ball

In learning to dribble, the first skill to develop is the ability to run quickly with the ball under your control. Generally, the laces or outside of the foot are used to gently push the ball quickly ahead of you. They are the easiest parts of the foot to use without breaking stride. As you run, keep the ball close, never letting it stray more than a yard or so from your feet. Always try to keep your head up to scan the field for opportunities to make a good pass.

Once that technique is mastered, try faking out defenders. The key to escaping defenders is to get them to commit their body weight in one direction, left or right, then drive with the ball the other way. The easiest technique for doing this is the body swerve: Move toward the defender, trying not to diminish your speed excessively, while keeping the ball under your firm control. When the defender is barely out of tackling range, step with your, let's say, left foot, planting it behind and well to the left of the ball. Lean *dramatically* to the left with your shoulders and upper body.

An overeager defender will lunge to stop your leftward move; as they are doing so, use the top of your right foot to push the ball forward and to the right, past the helpless back foot of the defender. Now accelerate into open space.

Making the feint believable.

The defender falls for the feint and the ball is pushed past his trailing foot.

Here's a variation on this maneuver that may momentarily put you off-balance. But the quickness with which this move can be accomplished more than makes up for it. Dip your shoulder while stepping all the way over the ball in the direction of the dip, with the foot on the opposite side from your dipped shoulder. It will now be perfectly poised to push the ball in the direction from which you have just stepped. The defender will have lunged and stepped in the direction of your shoulder dip, so just flick the ball past the defender's back foot, using the outside of your stepping foot. Now accelerate.

The fakes just described are two of the easiest, yet most effective ways to aggressively beat a defender.

A rollover to the left.

A flick to the right.

A "nutmeg."

Another useful ploy is to try a dramatically acted out fake kick. This can be done by drawing your kicking leg back and swinging it, but stopping short of the ball. Then the instant after the defender stabs out a foot to block the kick, or even flinches, flick the ball right between his or her outspread legs and accelerate away.

Other useful tricks are a simple, sudden deceleration with the ball, or a sudden acceleration just as the defender arrives to tackle the ball away.

Keeping the defender the maximum distance from the ball.

Shielding the Ball

Sometimes it's better to just keep control of the ball, or even slow the pace of the game, to give time for your teammates to arrive and help out. Luckily, you needn't always confront and fake out the defender but can simply plant your body between defender and ball. Keep your weight low and your arms slightly out for balance, shielding the ball. If the defender is approaching from the right, for example, control the ball on your left foot. If the defender is directly on top of you, don't give in to the temptation to completely turn your back. Try to stay sideways with the ball on the foot farthest away from the threatening opponent, denying him or her any chance to poke at it through your legs. When you shield correctly, your opponent will not be able to get to the ball without fouling you. He or she will become impatient and, breathing down your neck, will be tempted to sneak around one side or the other to try to get at the ball. If you stay calm you'll actually be able to feel an opponent doing it. When you do, just pivot quickly in the same direction your opponent is moving, bringing the ball with you and giving your opponent only your shoulder that is off the ball; then when he is overcommitted to the wrong side, accelerate away with the ball.

There are an infinite number of ways to dribble, and it's fun to invent your own. As long as you don't let it become the most important part of your game, it will definitely make you a better player.

The defender tries to sneak around . . . . . . and in doing so gives his opponent a way out.

5 Tackling

Good defense requires many skills: marking, which in most other sports is called guarding; jockeying, which means to stall and get your opponent to move in the direction you want; moving to support teammates; as well as the most obvious one, tackling. Tackling is the art of taking the ball from your opponent either by simply knocking it away and creating a loose ball, or stealing it for yourself. Of all these, the most difficult skill may well be not simply tackling, but *timing* the tackle. As we learned in the last chapter, as your opponent advances he or she will constantly try to fake you out and force you to commit yourself at the wrong time or in the wrong direction. If you do mistime your tackle, you'll end up lying, very conspicuously, flat on your back, your opponent scoring while you wipe the egg from your face.

Once you decide that the moment is right, boldness is called for. You must give your all when you tackle your opponent. You may well end up with a bruise or a scrape instead of the ball, but that's just the way it is in soccer.

Don't be discouraged. Despite all the emphasis on ball control, it's important to remember that it is a most rare and difficult thing in soccer for a team to control the ball from one end of the field to the other and then score. It is, on the other hand, the most common of occurrences for a team to lose control of the ball, and a little concerted effort from you and your teammates makes it extremely likely that the opposing team will.

Basic Tackling Principles

The techniques of tackling are many: standing blocks, side blocks, shoulder charges, sliding tackles, and dozens of variants of each. All, when executed properly, share a few principles:

- When you can, you must assume a poised stance, weight low on the balls of the feet and feet shoulder width apart. Keep your eyes on the ball. You might monitor the hips of the attacker for an early indication of where the attacker is headed—but primarily, you watch the ball.
- Stay "goalside" of the attacker, meaning that you keep yourself between the attacker and the goal that's being attacked. In that position, the opponent must either shoot the ball through you, or dribble around you to directly attack your goal. Also, by staying goalside of the attacker, a defender is able to steer an opponent with the ball away from the goal and toward the sideline, where the opponent can do much less damage than he or she could do in front of the goal. If you can force an opponent with the ball into a harmless position, you've won the duel without ever having touched the ball.

- Stay within striking distance when opponents have the ball. This means not so close that they can be easily bypassed, but yet not so cautiously far away that attackers have time to do whatever they want.
- When the odds are in your favor, try to intercept the ball before the attacker ever has a chance to touch it. Failing that, try to tackle while the opponent is concentrating on bringing the ball under control. If *that* doesn't work, try to prevent the attacker from turning with the ball so that he or she is facing the goal.

Front Tackle

You and your opponent are moving directly toward each other. As you move in to tackle, place most of your weight on your planted, nontackling foot, and lean with your shoulder on that side of the body and toward your opponent's chest. This will bring your body weight forward. The inside of your tackling foot, with the toes turned slightly up and ankles locked, makes contact with the center of the ball much like it would if you were making an inside-of-the-foot pass. The knee of your tackling leg will be directly over the ball. Your weight being forward and low will give you a great advantage in leverage if both you and your opponent make contact with the ball at the same time. If this happens, *keep* your weight low so you will have more leverage on the ball than your opponent and try to push, pull, or poke with your foot—anything necessary to pry the ball clear.

Little follow through will be necessary, since the motion of your tackling leg is somewhat downward on the ball.

Player No. 4 is making a strong tackle.

Sliding Tackle

Preparing to make a sliding tackle.

The sliding tackle—impressive, daring, and very effective—is the one tackle you should avoid if there are any other options available that would allow you to remain standing. The reason is that the sliding tackle leaves you flat on your back. If you miss making the tackle, you've accomplished nothing except rendering yourself temporarily useless to your team in the face of a developing attack. If, however, it is the *only* tackle that will work when you *must* stop an attacker breaking clear with the ball, then by all means use it.

You may employ a sliding tackle straight on, from the side, or as you overtake an opponent, but not from behind, which would be a foul. As you overtake an escaping opponent, swing your leg (the leg farthest from the ball's path) across the path of the ball, while at the same time dropping to the

Down, but it's his opponent who's out of the play.

ground and sliding on the calf of the leg nearest your opponent. As you sweep your tackling leg around from the far side, keep it in contact with the ground. Swing from the knee as you kick the ball away with the laces of your shoe, making sure to send it around and behind your opponent. If you hit the ball into your opponent's legs, it will simply rebound off your opponent, over you, and he'll continue on his way. Get up immediately.

The timing of this tackle is very difficult, and it can be dangerous for both players. It is particularly important to make sure you do not slide into your opponent from *behind*. This is not only one of the most dangerous fouls in soccer, but it could get you ejected from the game.

Side Tackle

If you are approaching an opponent at a right angle and want to do more than poke the ball away, try to gain control of the ball and transform this opportunity into a front tackle situation. Do this by planting your nontackling foot near and slightly in front of your opponent. Pivot on your planted, nontackling foot, rotating the inside of your tackling foot (with a locked ankle) into the center of the ball as you lower your shoulder.

Timing will be more difficult than with the front tackle, since your opponent can put on a quick burst of speed and leave you badly out of position. However, depending on what your opponent sees peripherally, you may well have the all-important element of surprise on your side.

The defender approaching from the side . . .

. . . then turning into the tackle.

Shoulder Charge

You may be able to force your opponent into an error using the technique known as the shoulder charge. When running alongside an opponent with the ball, lean into him, pressing your shoulder (not your arm or elbow) against your opponent's shoulder, steering him off the ball. If you apply enough pressure and throw your opponent off-balance, you may force an error or get a chance for a touch of the ball.

Do not use this as an excuse to ram into your opponent at top speed. And remember, it is not legal to use anything but the shoulders. This technique is legal only when both players are close enough to the ball that they have a reasonable opportunity to play the ball during the charge. You cannot use the shoulder charge on a player who does not have possession of the ball.

A legal shoulder charge.

6 Special Skills

The specialist is very rare in soccer. Very few situations occur in soccer in which any player with a full range of good skills cannot perform perfectly well. There are, however, a few situations where some special knowledge and techniques are required. It may take some extra effort, but there is absolutely no reason not to practice these useful techniques. You will most certainly be called on to use these special skills in a game, and their correct execution will help you gain a major advantage over your opponents.

The Throw-In

When the ball goes out of bounds across the sideline, a throw-in puts it back into play. Decades ago, players could throw the ball in any way they liked. Throw-ins became a major advantage as the players learned to throw the ball great distances with pinpoint accuracy. To prevent this, the rules were changed, and the manner in which the ball could be thrown in was limited to the few obviously awkward motions that are allowed today.

Illegal throw-ins are very common rule infractions. Since such infringements cost a team the ball, before we can discuss how to make the throw-in a potent weapon, we should review the throw-in rules.

- Both hands must stay on the ball during the throwing motion.
- As you throw, the ball must pass continuously over your head and be released there. Your arms must follow through in the same direction as the throw. All this prevents you from faking during your actual throwing motion or from simply dropping the ball in bounds.
- You must face the field of play, and both feet should remain touching the ground until the ball has left your hands. Also, the ball must have left your hands before you step onto the field.

As the player taking the throw-in, your first priority is to quickly achieve ball control on the field. The fact that you can make a long and accurate *legal* throw will help you maintain control of the ball, but making the throw quickly is of prime importance whether your throw is long or short.

Take a comfortable stance with your feet roughly shoulder width apart, either parallel to each other or one in front of the other. Hold the ball at chest height and spread your fingers wide apart on both sides of the ball, making sure you have a good grip. When ready to throw, bend your knees and lean your trunk backward. At the same time, draw the ball up, over, and somewhat behind your head, cocking your shoulders, elbows, and wrists. At this point you are coiled, ready to throw.

Now straighten your body in a whipping motion, starting with your knees, then body, arms, and finally your wrists, as you release the ball. The point above where you release the ball will determine its trajectory. The farther back behind the head the release, the higher the trajectory; a later release, farther to the front, will result in a lower arc on the throw.

As you follow through in the direction of the throw, your weight shifts to your toes. Once you become comfortable with this technique, you can add a short run-up to increase your distance slightly.

Wind-up for a long throw.

Putting the whole body behind the throw.

Defensive Wall

When your opponents are awarded a free kick near your goal, it is imperative that you set up a barrier of players to block a direct shot at your goal. At that range a free kick could easily result in a score. No special techniques are required to stand in a defensive wall, but it does take some bravery; you could very possibly be smacked silly by a hard shot. Remember to face the shooter to avoid kidney injury and to cover up vulnerable parts. However, what does require special knowledge is the technique of setting up the wall.

A field player is designated wall captain before the game. This keeps the goalkeeper from having to take time during the emergency to arrange the wall. He's free to get set for a quick shot right away.

It's the wall captain's responsibility to work with the goalkeeper to get the wall in the right place and get the right number of players in it. As wall captain, the moment the free kick is awarded, you should position yourself between the ball and the goalpost nearest it. The rules say you must be at least ten yards away from the ball; if you undercalculate a bit and are too close, don't worry, the ref will let you know.

Position yourself to slightly overcover the near post by checking back and forth between ball and post, imagining the line between the two. Meanwhile, you should be calling whatever number of preselected teammates you think you need to join you in the wall. A free kick from directly in front of the goal may require five or even six wall members, while a free kick from farther away or way off to the side should only require three.

Whatever its size, this barrier is designed to give the goalkeeper less goal to cover and should shield approximately half the goal mouth, leaving the back half under the keeper's protection.

Your wallmates will line up shoulder to shoulder, extending the wall toward the center of the goal. You might even enlist an extra teammate to charge the ball after it is first touched. Remember, as the play develops, the wall members must break away and resume their regular defensive behavior. They should do this as soon as the ball movement renders the wall superfluous.

Penalty Kicks

A penalty kick is soccer's punishment for a team that commits a serious foul in front of its own goal mouth. The kick is not taken with any particularly special technique. The ball is struck just as it would be for any other shot. What is different about this kick is the amount of pressure on the kicker, who is expected to make the shot every time. For this reason, penalty kicks should be practiced very differently from other soccer skills.

To practice the penalty kick, set one ball after another on the penalty stripe and kick them over and over to the same spot; preferably in the lower left or lower right hand corner of the goal. Give the kick the same degree of moderate to fast speed and use the same number of steps to approach each kick. Develop the ability to send the ball to the same spot again and again by rote, without thinking. Then, in the game, kick your penalty exactly this way. It's really not necessary to practice against the goalkeeper; the proper mind-set is not that you're out to beat the goalkeeper, but that you are going to hit your tried and true, consistently placed, unstoppable shot. Once you've switched your focus to the goalkeeper, you're halfway to making an error. Remember, far more penalty scoring opportunities are lost from missed shots than from goalkeeper saves.

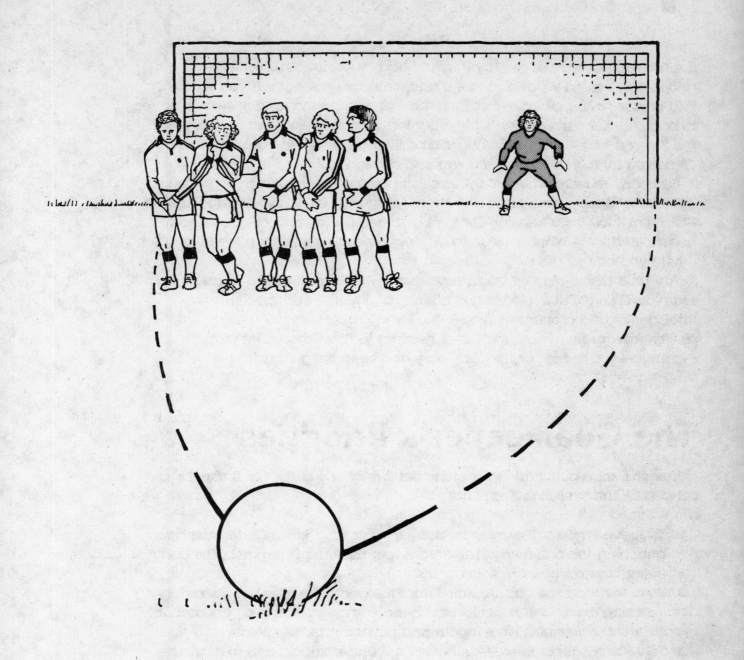

The wall covering the near half of the goal.

7 Goalkeeping

Even if you never hope to play in goal, read on. Knowledge of the goalkeeper's mind-set and tactics is an invaluable asset when you suddenly find yourself in front of the goal with the ball on your foot and only one player to beat: the keeper. Besides, when your team's goalkeeper comes down with the flu, you never know who might be called on to step in front of the net. Once you try it, you'll find it a rewarding challenge.

Early one season, when all the starting positions were still up for grabs, a coach asked me which player he ought to try to develop into the goalkeeper. I told him, "Ask your best athlete to play there. During a close game, he's guaranteed to be worth two goals. There's no other position on the field where you can say that."

An athletically talented goalkeeper *is* one of the most valuable assets a team can have. But in addition to athletic ability, the position demands intelligence and proper technique. The best goalkeepers use their athletic ability only rarely, when absolutely necessary. They know that proper techniques make the position look easy and keep the goal safe.

The Goalkeeper's Priorities

Keeping shots out of the back of the net is only one of the goalkeeper's concerns. The overall priorities are

1. To prevent goals. This must be done by catching, kicking, deflecting, or punching the ball away. The goalkeeper may use any part of the body, including hands or arms, to do this.
2. To prevent dangerous rebounds near the goal. This is done by securely *catching* every ball possible, and *punching* or *deflecting* all uncatchable balls away from the goal mouth and out of immediate play.
3. To verbally direct the defense when it is under attack, and to distribute the ball effectively to teammates after catching it. Your team is never in a surer position with the ball than when it is in the goalkeeper's hands. This makes the goalkeeper's distribution a very versatile tool.
4. To play every ball as easily, properly, and confidently as possible, and to dominate the entire penalty area. This will inspire confidence in your team. Free from anxiety at their backs, they will all play a better game.

Positioning

Each of these priorities involves, in one way or another, handling the ball. Remember, the penalty area and goal mouth are large compared to a single person, and unless you keep yourself in a position where you can reach the ball, you won't even be able to handle it much less keep it from the goal. It is therefore very important if you are going to develop the techniques of catching the ball that you first develop the technique of proper positioning.

Many novice goalkeepers take up a position on their own goal line, and remain there for the better part of the game. This is the position they are required to take up for a penalty, and it's a long way to jump to either goalpost.

In order to take up a more advantageous position, you should take a few steps off the goal line toward the attacker who has the ball. You will look much bigger and visually block more of the goal from the attacker. More importantly, if you imagine two lines running from the ball to touch the right and left posts, you can easily see that any ball traveling toward your goal within those lines is a potential score. You can also see that as you move out off the goal line toward the ball, you have less and less distance to cover if you must dive to either side to stop a shot. Imagining this triangle is very useful.

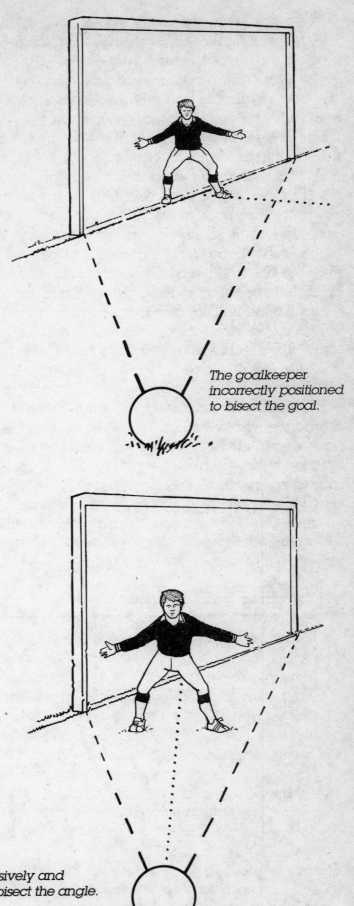

The goalkeeper incorrectly positioned to bisect the goal.

The goalkeeper aggressively and correctly positioned to bisect the angle.

Every ball on every part of the field will create one of these triangles. Some from way off on the side of the field make narrow triangles that are easy to block without moving far from the goal. Others from right in front of the goal make wider triangles that force you to come farther out, away from the goal line and toward the ball, somewhere along the rounded outer part of the oval. When covering angles on different shots, your movements will more or less resemble an oval in front of the goal, stretching to either post and out to the six-yard line. The flat back part of the oval is for corner kicks and wide-angle shots, since the biggest problem for you in these instances is that these are not direct shots, but passes into the center from the wing.

You may wonder, since the farther out you go the easier it is to cover the angle, why not go all the way out to the ball? There are two reasons. First, a fullback should be filling that role. Second, you need to stay far enough away from the ball to have time to react and protect the goal. The goal can be protected either by blocking the shot, backing up under a chip, repositioning yourself if the ball is passed, or smothering the ball at the feet of an opponent who has gotten too close. Remember, it doesn't matter if the ball streaks by "only" three inches from your hand if you don't have time to move your hand and stop it.

Generally, the key is to advance out as far as you can while still allowing enough room for ample reaction time. However, your opponents might create a situation where they can get so close with the ball that you simply will not have enough time to react to a shot. Since they have denied you your reaction time, you must deny them their shooting angle—all of it. Do this by remaining aware of the angle and moving immediately in one motion right down the middle of it, all the way to the ball at their feet. Then, no matter what shot the forward tries, the ball is bound to hit you. More on this technique later.

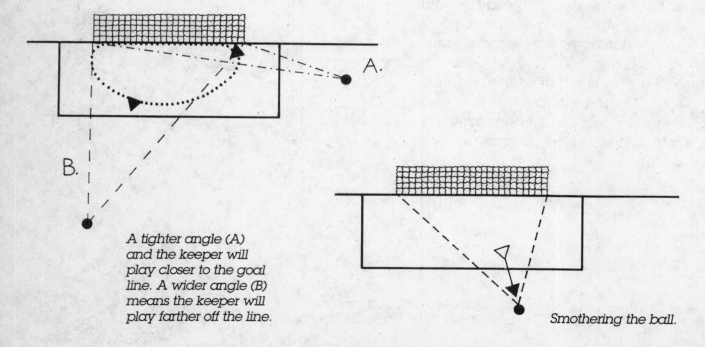

A tighter angle (A) and the keeper will play closer to the goal line. A wider angle (B) means the keeper will play farther off the line.

Smothering the ball.

Stance

There is a poised "ready position" for goalkeeping that serves as a generally effective position from which you can quickly do anything that is demanded. This position is the basis for all ball catching and diving techniques.

To assume the ready position, directly face the ball, keep your body weight forward, your heels slightly off the ground, feet shoulder width apart. Bend at the knees and waist so that you're coiled and ready to spring. Don't waste time crouching to spring after the ball has been shot; be prepared beforehand by already having your knees bent and rear end low. Your hands should be relaxed, held slightly out from the body and down with palms facing the shooter.

In the course of a game, as you adjust your position around the goal mouth, your feet should be moving primarily in a quick shuffle. When there's danger, always maintain your stance, use short balanced steps, and avoid crossing your feet when changing position.

Ready position.

Catching

Catching the ball safely, securely, and consistently is a prerequisite for good goalkeeping. For goalkeepers, catching techniques are fundamental. Catch well and you change serious threats against your goal into quick, effective counterattack opportunities for your team. Catch poorly, allowing the ball to deflect off you, and you'll find yourself in a mad scramble on your own goal line with a good chance of getting injured or giving up a goal.

BASIC CATCHING PRINCIPLES

Many different catching techniques exist for each type of shot. The basic principles of good catching hold true for all of them.

- Make all catches facing the ball.
- All catches should be attempted using two hands. Watch the ball all the way into your hands.
- All catches should be made with the fingers. The fingers are spread apart and the hands and wrists remain supple, not rigid.
- All catches require you to absorb some of the force of the shot by drawing the arms slightly back toward the body.
- Attempt all catches so that as much of your body as possible is between the ball and the goal. Then, if the ball slips through, it won't go into the goal but will hit your body instead.
- Protect the ball after the catch by drawing it into your chest.

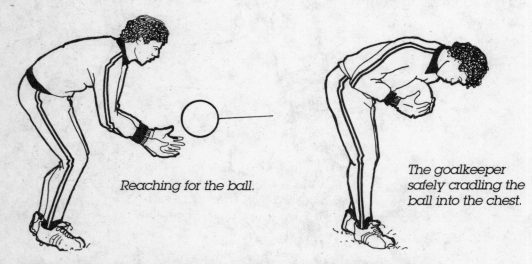

Reaching for the ball.

The goalkeeper safely cradling the ball into the chest.

CATCHING "AT THE BODY"—KNEE TO CHEST HEIGHT

Remain in a ready position. As the ball arrives, reach toward it with two hands, palms facing up. Your little fingers should be almost touching. As the ball arrives in your hands, draw your arms back slightly. This cushions and guides the ball to your chest. However, if the shot is extremely forceful, your hands will only have enough time to trap the ball into your chest. When the ball hits you there, you won't be able to reach out and cushion its force.

CATCHING AT OR ABOVE THE HEAD

When a ball is arriving at the goal above your head, it's very important to get both hands between the incoming ball and the goal, since above your head there can be no "body wall" behind the hands to back you up in case of error. Keep your hands and wrists relaxed as you reach up. They should be slightly forward of your head. Form a "w" beyond the ball with your thumbs and index fingers. If you must jump to reach the ball, use the one-footed takeoff described in chapter 3. As the ball arrives, cushion its impact by giving a little with your wrists and forearms. When you feel the ball securely in your hands, bring the ball down, securely clutching it to your chest.

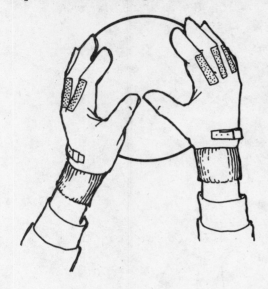

The "w" grip; the ball cannot push its way through.

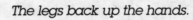

The legs back up the hands.

STOPPING SHOTS AT YOUR FEET

It is very important that in picking up ground balls you use a kneeling barrier. Balls rolling along the chewed-up ground of a well-used penalty area can take any number of strange hops.

From a ready position, step across the line of travel of the incoming ball. Plant your lead foot at a 90-degree angle across its path. Bend the trailing knee, touching it to the heel of the lead foot and the ground. Starting with outreaching fingertips just brushing the ground, scoop up the ball with both hands. Allow the momentum of the ball to roll it up into your chest as you wedge it in safely against your chest with your hands and forearms. If the ball were to take a bad hop, it would still hit a leg, knee, foot, or your body.

This is also an easy technique to perform on the move and provides a better view of the field than the old standing scoop technique.

The wrists and forearms "give" to absorb the force.

Crosses

When an opponent who is out on the edge of the field kicks a high ball across the mouth of the goal, it presents you with a special challenge. When a ball is "crossed" in this way, your opponents will have time to run under the ball and contest you for it. The flight-line of a high ball, often crossed from the side of the field, is a complex curve. Often the ball drops straight in at you, so it's very difficult to visually appraise its speed or height. You could easily find yourself out of position, which is why you must always first take a moment to evaluate the flight of the ball and determine exactly where it's going. Then you decide to go out to catch it or await developments in your goal mouth. Stick to your decision! If you begin running into position immediately when the ball is struck, you will be judging a moving ball with a moving field of vision. That will make judging the ball much more difficult. You may find you've made a wrong decision and get caught halfway.

After the momentary pause for judgment, if you decide to catch the cross, loudly let your teammates know you are going for it. You'll have a hard enough time fighting your opponents for the ball. You don't want to have to crawl over the backs of your teammates, too.

Then, move quickly into the line of flight of the ball. When you jump, convert your lateral motion into vertical height by using a one-footed takeoff. As you jump, your nontakeoff knee should be raised to add further height to the jump and provide you with some defense from jostling opponents who are trying to head the ball. Catch the ball at the highest possible point, with your arms outstretched above and in front of your head. Use the "w" grip, the same technique you used for high shots. Catching the ball high is important because you don't want to let an opponent head the ball. Your arms will give you almost a two-foot height advantage, so jump up with confidence. After catching it securely, immediately protect the ball by cradling it to your chest.

Diving Saves

The ability to make a fearless diving save is what many people admire most in a goalkeeper. However, it would be much better, if it were possible, to play the entire game standing up. To keep on your feet the whole game, though, your angle play would have to be so good that the ball seemed to come to you by magnetic attraction. Only the coach and a few knowledgeable players would appreciate the extremely high value of those safe, "easy" standing catches you were making.

One of the reasons it would be preferable to remain upright is that by doing so you keep your balance, have a good view of the field, and are ready to move wherever you're needed. In contrast, the diving save leaves you on the ground, out of position and temporarily out of the play. Depending on the result of your efforts, you may have another one of those seven-player mad scrambles on the goal line raging over your head.

In the real world, no matter how good your angle play, you will be forced to make diving saves. Think of them as diving interceptions, in the manner of American football. When diving, always try to use two hands to catch any shot that is possible to catch, so you can avoid further trouble by putting an end to the play right there. Don't give in to the temptation to settle for a one-handed deflection, using your trailing hand to break your fall. Think of yourself as practicing a specialized form of *catching*.

There are two basic types of diving saves. One is an all-out launch of your body through the air to intercept shots that are roaring toward a distant goalpost. The other is for low balls that you might dive right over if you dove all-out.

Both techniques share some common elements that you must employ to make a successful interception.

- Start from a standard ready position.
- Take a few quick stutter steps toward the ball if you have time and if you need them to reach the ball. Always face the ball throughout the entire dive/catch/landing.
- Involve both hands in the catch as soon as possible, forming a "w" grip and keeping your elbows in and not protruding to the sides.
- After you've caught the ball using proper catching technique, direct it downward. Your near side or low hand will be behind it and your far side or high hand will be on top.

LANDING

- Use this ball trapping technique not only to help control the ball but also to cushion your fall. Don't slam the ball down to the ground, *place* it gently, allowing your forearm, your side, and the side of your thigh to follow it in that order, landing and cushioning your fall.
- After quickly cradling the ball safely to your chest, get up immediately and look for passing opportunities.

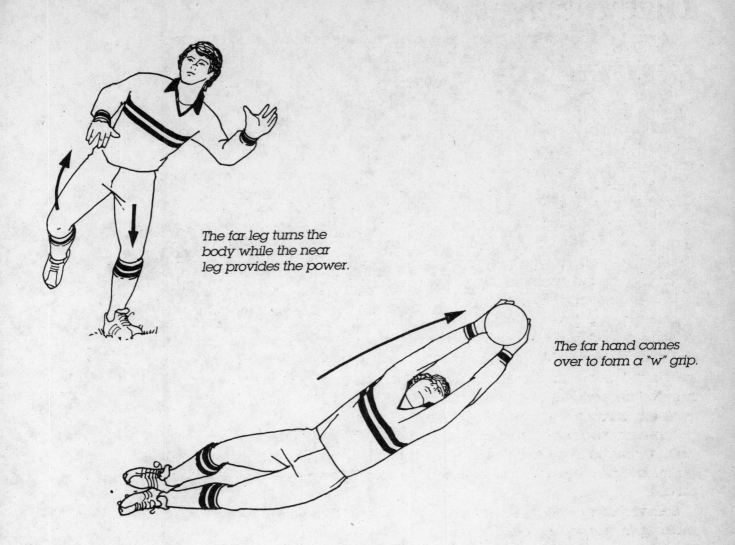

The far leg turns the body while the near leg provides the power.

The far hand comes over to form a "w" grip.

A safe landing on his side, with elbows in and body facing the field.

FULL STRETCH DIVE

Beyond the basics of diving, it is primarily the variations in footwork that make the different dives unique. The full stretch is a dive that you will employ when the ball seems to be well out of your reach.

As the shot approaches the goal, you should already be crouched and waiting in the ready position. The far side knee is raised up and across your body, followed an instant later by a powerful driving thrust by your other, near side leg. The shift of the far side leg will turn you sideways, while the thrust of the near leg will propel your body across the goal mouth. Standard diving, catching, and landing techniques are used after that point.

Remember, you've traveled a long way up and over in the air, but it is not yet time to start thinking about a landing. If you turn to face the turf, you will eliminate your view of the ball. You won't be able to save anything, and you will have turned your diving efforts into theatrics for the fans. You will also have exposed your elbows, stomach, wrists, and knees to injury when you hit. Proper diving and catching techniques are not only your most effective bet, but your safest one.

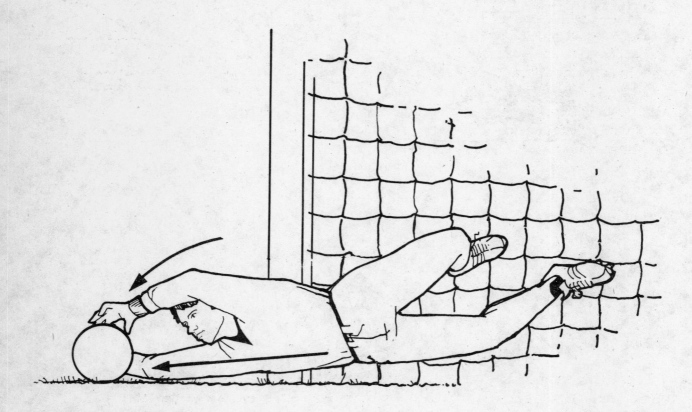

The near hand shoots out while the far hand reaches over.

GROUND LEVEL INTERCEPTIONS

The type of dive described above could send you sailing right over a ground ball.

In stretching to reach a distant ground ball, you must still use the knee thrust and still push off with your near side foot, but in this case the push off, as you lean in the direction you want to go, is primarily with the side of the foot. Now, rather than both hands being placed behind the ball as it arrives, the hand nearest the ball should shoot out *along the ground*. At the same time, the far hand comes over the top, free to control even a ball that hits a divot in a chewed-up penalty area and bounces up off the turf.

If the ball comes well within your range, take care not to dive right over it. Just let your leg nearest the ball relax and collapse its knee right out in front of you. The weight of your body, led by your hands and forced over by your far leg thrust, will very quickly bring your body wall and hands down to where they need to be.

She gets her near leg out of the way quickly . . .

. . . so she can get her body down behind the ball as soon as possible.

Smothering the Ball

To smother the ball at your opponent's feet requires more bravery than any other action in soccer. You should smother the ball when it appears that the opponent with the ball is taking a position so close to you that you will have no time to react until the ball is well on its way into the goal. Remember, if you fail to time your move correctly, your opponent will be able to score easily. But if you've developed the techniques for the diving save, you'll be well on the way to successful smothering, too.

The goalkeeper moving directly
to the ball, hands at the near post.

A body wall to prevent a goal.

Immediately upon realizing that the attacker is going to be too close, begin moving toward your opponent, bisecting the angle of all possible shots on goal. Once you've made the decision to go, you are committed to go all the way. If you change your mind halfway there, you'll neither smother your opponent nor will you be able to react and dive for the ball. In that case, just about any shot will score.

As you move forward, watch for any momentary error or loss of concentration on your opponent's part, and when you see it, instantly strike. Move to the ball and, as you arrive, lay down a body wall, using the same technique you do when diving for short ground balls. Imagine that you're going to use this body wall to sweep right through the ball.

As you lay down the wall, your forward motion will allow you to slide your legs and body along the ground, preventing your opponent from moving the ball toward the middle of the field. This will seal any move to the dangerous center of the field and force the attacker toward the less dangerous outside edge of the field and your waiting arms. Keep both your elbows in and flexed, reaching for the ball in front of your head. Your head should be well down behind those arms so that even if you fail to control the ball and the attacker's shooting foot deflects it away and follows through, you'll get just a foot to the forearm rather than a knee to the temple.

Hold on to the ball whenever you can, and do not swat the ball away when you arrive. This will prevent you from having to make the same save again two seconds later. Additionally, the ball provides you with excellent protection from direct blows to the head.

Deflecting and Punching

Sometimes, you may be jostled by opponents or stretched to your limits, or the shot you are fielding may be a real screamer on a wet or icy day. These are all particularly difficult situations in which to catch the ball, and a missed catch, which drops at an opponent's feet so he can easily kick it into the goal, is clearly much more disagreeable than a ball sailing out of your penalty area and away from danger. So it is sometimes wiser to redirect or deflect the ball away from danger rather than to catch it and risk dropping it.

Two ways to achieve this for two different situations are: punch high crosses that are dropping into your penalty area, and deflect powerful or hard to reach shots.

PUNCHING

Always try to use two fists to punch the ball if you can. Use a short, sharp jabbing motion, starting with your poised fists at eye level. Do not use a roundhouse swing. Hit the ball in the center of its underbelly, sending it high and giving you and your mates time to recover and reposition. Also, send the ball as far to the side of the field as you can with the direction of your jab and

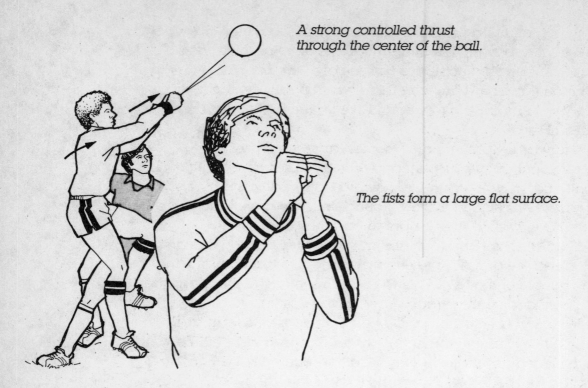

A strong controlled thrust through the center of the ball.

The fists form a large flat surface.

follow through. This eliminates the danger of an immediate shot when the ball comes down. Use a one-fisted punch only when you cannot reach the ball with both fists.

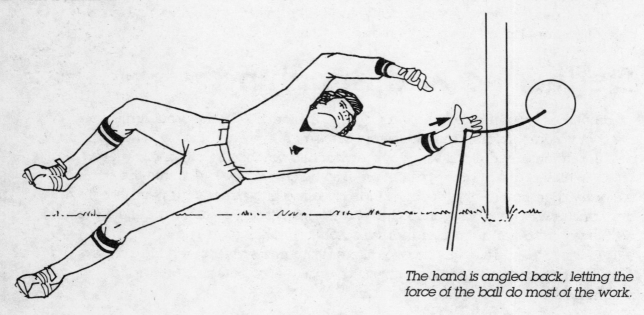

The hand is angled back, letting the force of the ball do most of the work.

DEFLECTING THE BALL

When a shot is just too hard to catch or is just too far away to catch with two hands, use your palms (both if possible) to deflect the ball. Turn them back at a slight angle toward the goal and allow the force of the shot to carry itself around the upright or over the crossbar and out of play at the back. You will be giving away a corner kick but buying time for your defense to set up. Under no circumstances should you try to block or swat a shot back into play.

A high ball, dropping over the keeper's head.

Tipping the ball over the bar with the high hand.

    If the ball is dropping into the goal over your head, you'll need to backpedal while continuing to face the field of play. As the ball nears, raise your hand nearest the ball with a sharp firm thrust and drive upward at the back center of the ball so that it is redirected up. Propelled by its own momentum and your follow through, it sails out the back over the crossbar. A one-handed fisting technique should be used only for a ball dropping from a particularly great height.

Distribution

As a goalkeeper, your job is not over once you've caught the ball. While the ball is still safely in your hands, your team is free to begin to launch a powerful counterattack. You will make the first pass in that attack. You can use a kick, throw, or roll—each method is best for a given situation. Rolling is good for a team that is confident and wants to maintain its ball control; kicking is best for a very quick counterthrust. But unlike a throw, a kicked ball is much more of a fifty-fifty proposition when it finally lands near midfield. However you choose to distribute the ball, all choices except long kicks should be made toward the sides, not up the middle of the field directly in front of your own goal. You should balance the force necessary to get the ball to your teammates quickly against the receiver's need to easily and quickly control the ball.

A punt, dropped out of the hands and kicked before it hits the ground, will travel very far but also quite high, giving both teams a chance to run under it, into its line of flight, and control it. In punting, follow the procedure for an instep volley. Remember to drop the ball from two hands and keep it well out in front of you, giving your kicking leg room to swing freely.

A drop kick is set up by dropping the ball out of the hands just like a punt, but is kicked just as it hits the ground. It's a quick, low, accurate kick. In drop kicking, follow the directions for the instep drive. When practicing, imagine you are kicking an instep drive. With this vivid picture in mind, the timing of your kick will take care of itself after only a few hundred practice kicks into the net.

Step toward the target . . .

. . . and involve the whole body when rolling the ball.

Every muscle participates in the throw. The elbow remains straight.

The whole body is cocked.

The roll and baseball throw are as accurate as they are self-explanatory. Always remember to step toward your target with the leg opposite your throwing arm. Keep your fingers well spread on the ball. You can roll the ball just as if you were bowling, but *don't* do it on a muddy field or the ball may die right in front of you in the mud.

One of the most useful distribution passes is the catapult-style throw. It can travel farther than any other throw but retains some of the greater accuracy of the more controlled baseball throw and so is often better than kicking.

Plant your body sideways to your target. Let's say a winger is forty yards upfield. With your nonthrowing shoulder pointing toward your target, keep the ball trapped between your throwing hand, which is behind the ball with fingers spread, and your wrist. Lower your rearward throwing shoulder, cocking your arm way back until the ball is at hip height. In catapulting the ball forward, your arm should come almost directly over the top with a stiff, unbent elbow. Your arm will pass right by your head and you'll release the ball just as it is slightly past that point.

Try to impart backspin, not sidespin, on the ball since this will increase your ability to control the ball and hence your accuracy.

8 Tactics

Technique is only one aspect of the multidimensional game of soccer. Conditioning, strategy, psychology, and tactics also play major parts.

As in any other team sport, having perfect technique and executing it flawlessly is of limited value unless you and your teammates have the necessary tactical insight and skill. During a game, it is through tactics that you reap the benefits of your skill. There are many variations on the basic attacking and defensive tactical ploys of a soccer team. The fluid nature of soccer makes it a certainty that these variations will be employed on many parts of the field throughout the game. The basic tactical tips presented in this chapter are in no way a conclusive tactical manifesto. Rather, as a primer it should help you more effectively execute the techniques you've practiced. The key is to choose your tactics wisely, appropriately, and creatively for the particular situation you are facing.

With no opposition at his back . . .

. . . the receiver turns quickly and moves downfield.

Tactical Tips

- As you develop ball trapping skill, learn to take most of the pace off the ball as you turn toward your opponents' goal in the same motion. Then it's off to the races before your opponent can even react.
- When coming to support a player with the ball, try to stand sideways to the player, facing your opponents' goal. This opens up both offensive and defensive passing possibilities in your immediate field of vision.

Shooting

- Defenses and goalkeepers are often caught flatfooted by a first-time shot. The penalty area is usually crowded, and in the time it takes you to trap the ball, the defenders can easily rob you of your chance to shoot. So even though it's a more difficult shot to hit accurately, don't be afraid to volley the ball at the goal from right out of the air, or shoot off the ground without trapping the ball first.

- Also, don't be afraid to try a long powerful shot from outside the penalty area. The shot itself may not yield a goal, but whatever shot you try, if your teammates are poised, ready to pounce on the ball when shots rebound off the keeper, you'll be surprised at the dividends this tactic can yield.

- All other things being equal, shoot low—it's the hardest shot for most goalkeepers to get to. The main thing to remember if you are close to the goal, however, is that at that range the keeper can only effectively defend the middle third of the goal, so just pick a side and shoot.

A better field of vision presents more passing options.

"Poaching"—taking advantage of the goalkeeper's error.

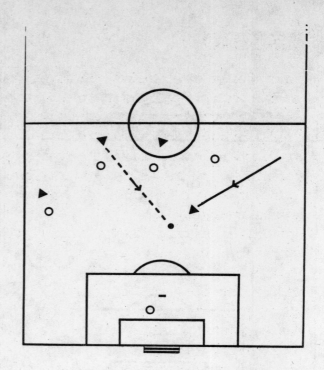

The most basic play in soccer.

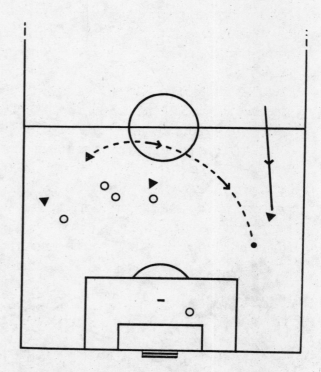

A through pass to a teammate breaking by the last line of defense.

●	Ball
▲	Attacker
○	Defender
- - -	Pass/Shot
——	Run
∿∿	Dribble

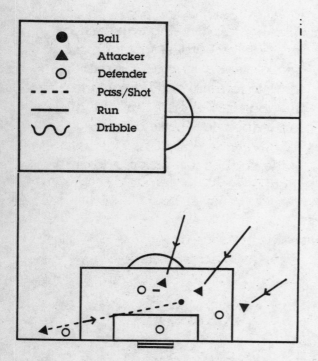

Passing back toward the onrushing attackers.

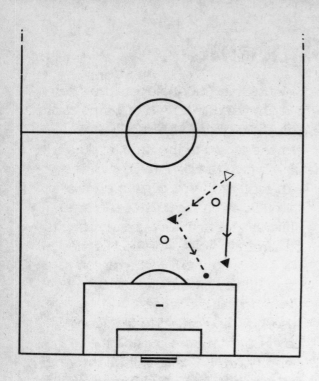

The left side is crowded, the right side isn't.

68

Passing

Sooner or later, as your game improves, you are going to need to take a greater risk with the ball and try to make a penetrating pass toward your opponents' goal. Since soccer is a ball possession game, make sure the gain from the pass is worth its extra riskiness.

- Fullbacks moving out of their own defense and goalkeepers should know that passes toward the edges of the field are less likely to lead to a dangerous turnover than passes up the middle, particularly when the goalkeeper wins the ball. The fullbacks should look to distribute it first toward the opposite side of the field, away from where the recent attack came from. This will be the least crowded sector of the field and so the best place to begin a counterattack.

- A nice, safe pass back to your goalkeeper is one of the best defensive plays you can make—don't be ashamed to use it. But remember to pass back slightly to the side of the goal mouth, not right at it.

- Use the simple but effective "wall pass" when you're confronted with a defender and you have teammates supporting you nearby, forward and to the side of your position. Pass the ball crisply to your mate, and spring past the defender. Your supporting teammate simply crisply and accurately kicks the ball into the space behind your defender, who is now in the unfortunate position of having to turn and try to catch you.

- Look for the opposing defense to become "flat" with all the fullbacks in a line straight across the field. Hit the ball through the gap between two of them, into the space behind them, at the same time as a teammate dashes past.

- While keeping in mind that controlling the ball is the name of the game, a team with good communication will find that a bit of one-touch passing in which they pass the ball without first trapping it will double the effectiveness of its passes and vary the rhythm of its play in a way that will keep defenders guessing.

- If you wait to cross the ball until you are on the end line, your teammates can run toward the oncoming ball and will have a much easier time heading it into the goal.

- If you are attacking a massed defense down one side of the field, consider a long high pass to the other side and an unopposed teammate.

Running Off the Ball on Attack

Players are taught early on that passing is the name of the game. But passing loses its point; indeed, there will be no possibility of passing whatsoever unless your team is in continual movement, running to get open for passes or lure defenders away from the ball.

When moving without the ball, it is important that you and your mates give your dribbling player as many safe passing options as you can—forward, square, and to the rear. Some players should be running away from the ball handler, spreading the defense and creating potential opportunities, others should be running toward the handler, getting close enough for safe passes. These roles will reverse frequently. The key concept here is "depth," far and near, forward, backward, left and right.

- Defenders want to watch both the ball and the attacking players that they are marking. So, if your defender overplays you watching the ball and hopes to intercept a pass or tries to support the defender attacking the ball, run forward, behind the back of your defender and out of his or her field of vision.
- All other factors being equal, the best location to support ball handlers is not behind or directly square to them, but behind and beside them at 45-degree angles.
- Speak up. Remember, the ball handler is very busy and can use any succinct one- or two-word bits of information you can deliver. "Turn . . . man on . . . now."
- If you are in a forward position and a teammate with the ball is having a good run headed toward the goal with his or her defender, move out of the way, clearing both yourself and your defender from the space your teammate needs. The last thing a ball carrier breaking free wants to run into is a crowd.
- Remember, diagonal runs are almost always better than straight-ahead ones. They prevent defenders who are covering the ball carrier from interposing themselves between the ball and the goal, simultaneously eliminating you from the play.

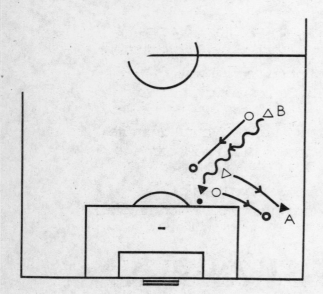

Player A gets out of B's way.

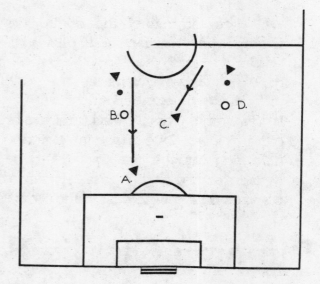

Player A has made an unproductive run; B can guard A and the ball. C has made a productive run. D must cover the ball and leave C open to receive a pass.

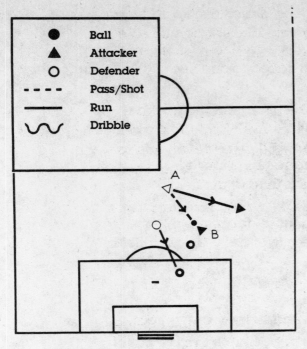

Legend:
● Ball
▲ Attacker
○ Defender
- - - - Pass/Shot
——— Run
〰〰 Dribble

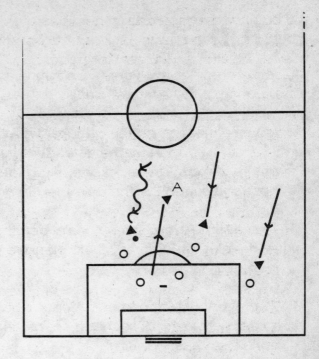

Player A passes, then runs to support B.   *Player A gets open by moving against the grain.*

As an attacking team, your short-term objectives are:

- To support the ball carriers, giving them as many passing options as possible. This will, at the very least, improve their dribbling opportunities.
- To pull defenders away from the front of their goal, opening this area to attack.
- To move in front of the opponents' goal only when you can shake your defender and your teammate has an opportunity to pass, or if you have the ball.
- Don't stand there admiring your good pass; one option is to follow your pass and support the player receiving it.
- Move into the space your teammates just left. You may well find yourself wide open.

Obviously you can develop penetrating possibilities if you run while others around you are walking. It's less obvious, but if you walk while others around you are running, you may find yourself forgotten about by the defense and wide open for a pass.

Along with communication with the ball handler, suddenly either quickening or lessening your pace or changing the timing of your run when your defender is distracted by the ball are the two most important tools for losing the defender who's marking you.

Defense

Goals scored against your team can usually be traced to one or a combination of these four reasons:

- too little pressure on the attacker with the ball;
- little or no support for the defender trying to pressure the ball;
- failure to mark an attacker moving into a threatening position;
- poor ball control by the defenders in your back third of the field.

Here are some tactical methods of dealing with these errors:

First, develop an orderly set of defensive priorities. Normally the priorities of the defending team are:

1. To prevent the immediate threat to their goal;
2. To delay the attack so that more of their teammates may arrive from upfield and help defend;
3. To disrupt the attack, making productive or creative activity with the ball difficult or impossible;
4. To win the ball;
5. To initiate a counterattack.

Marking is guarding a player. The opponent you are marking may or may not have the ball.

When marking the ball carrier, always position yourself between the carrier and the goal in a poised position, weight forward (even if you're forced to backpedal).

Your distance from the ball is a crucial consideration. You must be close enough to pounce on any mistake, but not so close that the ball can easily be flicked past you. Be prepared to change direction at a moment's notice. Don't let dribblers beat you with speed—force them to beat you with skill. If the dribbler is passing you on the wing, turn and run shoulder to shoulder with the dribbler, directing the dribbler into a tighter and tighter pinch on the sideline. Once there, you or you and a recovering teammate can snuff the threat out against the sideline. In the center, if not so near your goal that a quick change of direction will give your opponent a shot, try to slow the dribbler down by playing a few yards off until help arrives. Help may come either in the form of an extra defender behind you whose arrival will allow you to go ahead and tackle, or someone to ambush the dribbler from his or her blind side.

Your order of battle in dealing with your immediate opponent is:

- Prevent your player from getting the ball;
- Prevent your player from controlling the ball;
- Prevent your player from turning and facing the goal with the ball;
- Prevent your opponent from moving toward the center with the ball;
- *Never* let your opponent get between you and the goal with the ball.

Sooner or later the ball carrier may be so close to your goal that you must commit yourself to a desperate tackle, but until that time, don't sell yourself cheaply. Be patient and wait until you can choose the best opportunity to tackle.

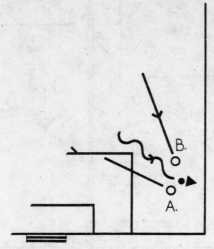

Player A steers the attacker to the sidelines, then B seals the trap.

Jockeying the ball-carrier toward the sideline.

Marking the Player Without the Ball

It is not necessary to follow an assigned attacker step for step; in fact, this is often a waste of energy. If the ball is not too near, stay well on the goalside but play off them some yards toward the ball; that way you can keep an eye on the attacker and the ball. This will increase your chances of intercepting the ball and also eliminate your opponent's opportunity to run behind you while you're watching the ball. It also leaves you free to support other defenders. You should only mark an opponent by fronting (interposing yourself between the opponent and the ball) when you have otherwise unoccupied defensive help behind you.

The closer the ball is to your sector of the field the less time you will have to react and tackle an opponent when he or she receives the ball—therefore, the closer you must mark. The last thing you want to do is to try to stop an opponent who has the ball and is traveling at full speed right at you.

When you're beaten by the player with the ball and you have a supporting defender behind you, you should turn and, taking the inside route, run back and become the support for the player who was recently supporting you.

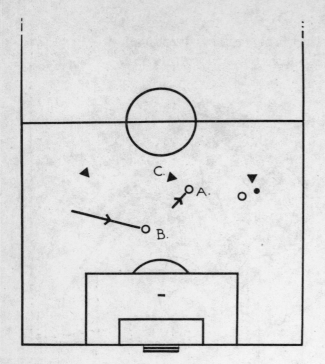

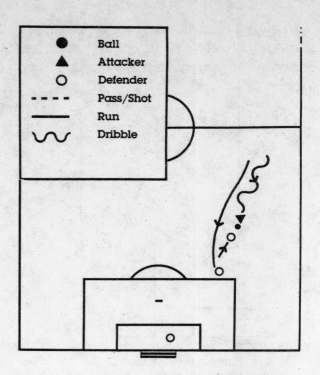

Legend:
● Ball
▲ Attacker
○ Defender
- - - - Pass/Shot
——— Run
〰〰 Dribble

Playing off attackers who are out of the play. Player A knows he can "front" C because B has moved in behind him for support.

Covering defensively for the player who covered for you.

Special Situations

Soccer presents many special situations—wet days, muddy fields, situations of ten versus eleven players, etc. Here are a few of them with some suggestions.

Wet days: On very wet days the ball is almost impossible to roll along the ground. Play long passes in the air in these conditions. Remember, the ball will be unruly and difficult to trap. All players, *but particularly the goalkeeper*, should take care to position themselves with their bodies behind the ball's line of flight.

Breakaways: Goalkeepers should try to dominate their penalty area and gain control of every ball they can. This includes receiving throw-ins and some free kicks near the penalty area. If the goalkeeper sees the threat of an opponent running past the defensive players to control a ball past them, he or she may move all the way out of the penalty area and kick or head the ball out of bounds, just as a fullback would. In this way, the goalkeeper eliminates the danger before it moves close to the goal mouth. Keepers should remember that on long through passes, they have the advantage that the ball is moving toward them, while forwards must catch up to it. A fullback should move into goal to cover the keeper's back.

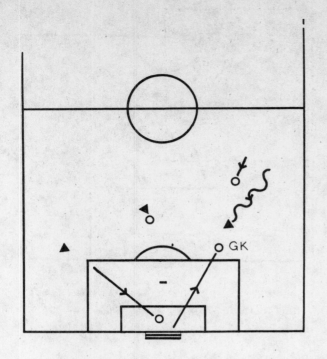

The fullback moves to
cover for the goalkeeper.

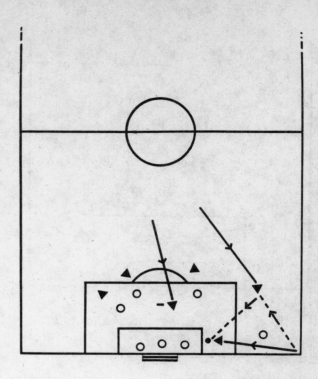

A short corner.

Corner kicks: On corner kicks, station two players just inside either goalpost. They're there not only to head curve shots away but to *step in* and cover the goal if the keeper moves out to catch the ball. Keepers should position themselves back from the center of the goal, since it is easier to run forward and catch a ball than it is to back up and do so. Attacking players should mix in a few short "give and go" type corners along with their usual long ones.

- The goalkeeper should feel no pressure during a penalty kick, but should just resolve to defend the middle third of the goal, forcing the kicker to score with a good kick. There are more poor penalty kicks than one would imagine, and the keeper should avoid the temptation to guess which side the kicker will try for before the ball is kicked.
- When forming a defensive wall, fullbacks should be left free to do what they do best—mark opponents. Forward players may be too far away to set up a wall quickly. This leaves the midfield players to form the wall. Since so many players will be occupied in the wall, the forwards *must* hurry back and help defend.
- It is best to put the ball into play quickly on a throw-in. If you have a long-throw specialist, great, use that ploy sometimes. However, it won't take any time at all for the defense to figure out what's coming when they see that player trotting across the field to take the throw.

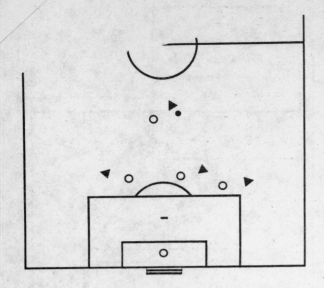

The forwards are straining the limits of the defense.

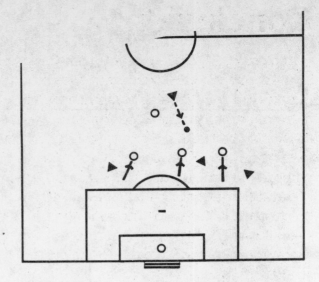

A few quick steps forward by the defenders and all of the opponents are offside.

The Offside Trap

If your opponents are consistently trying to kick through passes as their poised lead players try to dash past your last line of defense, it may be a good idea to try an offside trap.

This tactic depends on astute and observant referees and linesmen. The fact that your team likes to use this ploy might be mentioned in an appropriate manner to the referee by your coach or team captain before the game. Otherwise, if the ref misses the call, your team will end up with egg on their face at midfield while your opponents are swooping down unmolested on your goal.

First, it would be worth your time to look into the rule book and learn the offside rule. Very generally, it requires that players waiting to receive passes must keep two opponents between themselves and the goal they want to attack. The attackers may move past those two defenders once the ball is passed to them.

The trap: The defense can use the offside rule to their advantage, manipulating their positions to get the officials to call the attacking team "offside." At a prearranged word or signal from your goalkeeper or center fullback and just before your opponent hits a through pass, the entire defense should step forward upfield, leaving the attackers who are trying to break past the defense with only the goalkeeper between them and the goal—an offside position. You must practice this first before trying it in a game, because every defender must be willing to step up immediately. If even only one defender fails to do so, or if your timing is off, it won't work, and your defense will be caught flat, an easy victim for any number of attacking strategies. Remember, you're depending on the referee and linesman to make the offside call, so if you don't have confidence in them, the trap is too risky.

Conclusion

In closing, let me leave you with this: Like the soccer ball, soccer and soccer players are multifaceted entities. Ideally, there are no fullbacks, there are no forwards, there are only players. Each team member in the perfect team moves without the ball, creates, covers for, and communicates with all other teammates on all parts of the field. The more you keep this philosophy in mind and the more you play for enjoyment, the more your techniques will improve. And the more your techniques improve, the more you will enjoy the game and be able to implement the philosophy.

I hope this book has been helpful to you during practice. I also hope that you'll have great success and enjoy soccer for many years, as I have.

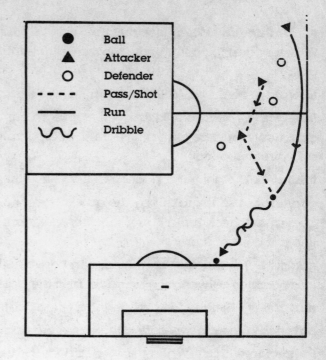

A long "overlapping" run has been made from the back, out of the defense.

Glossary

advantage law   This rule says that play may continue after a foul if continuing the play would be to the advantage of the side that was fouled against.

bend   To kick the ball and make it swerve, or curve, in flight.

center   To pass the ball into the middle of the field (usually the penalty area) from the side.

charge   Illegal body contact that knocks an opponent off the ball.

clear   To kick or head the ball clear of your goal area.

cross   To pass from a wide position to the center of the field near the goal.

defensive clearance   When a player sends a ball high and far away from his goal, usually in a hectic situation, to prevent the opponents from scoring.

direct free kick   The player who is given this kick is allowed to score by kicking the ball directly into the opponents' net.

distribution   Pass made by the goalkeeper.

dribbling   "Handling" the ball with the feet.

far post   The goalpost most distant from the player who has the ball.

first time   Playing the ball without pausing to trap or control it.

follow through   When kicking or throwing in the ball, allowing the kicking leg/throwing arm to continue the movement after the ball has been released or propelled away.

forward   A front line attacking player—for example, a striker or winger.

free kick   A dead-ball kick given to a team after their opponents break the rules. The opponents must be ten yards from the ball during the kick. See also **indirect free kick** and **direct free kick**.

fullback   The defender positioned nearest to the goal line.

goal kick   Usually taken by the goalkeeper or fullback, this kick is made from the goal area to restart play after the offensive team has played the ball over the goal line but has not scored.

goalside   For a defender, the position between the attacker and the goal; for the attacker, it is between the defender and the goal.

half volley   Kicking the ball on the first touch after it bounces.

hat trick   One player scoring three or more goals in one game.

indirect free kick   When this is awarded, the ball must touch at least two players before the team can score.

injury time   Extra time added to the play to make up for pauses for injury, goal scoring, or time wasting.

jockeying   A tactic in which a defender refrains from tackling an opponent immediately, trying instead to get that opponent to move in a disadvantageous direction or move the ball to his or her weaker foot.

juggling   Without using hands or arms, players practice preventing the ball from touching the ground.

kickoff   From the center of the court, this kick starts the game at the onset, or after halftime or a goal.

linesman   Official whose job it is to assist the ref.

lob   A short, high kick that aims at clearing an opponent's head.

mark   To guard an opponent; trying to keep the ball away from an opponent or keep him or her from doing anything productive with the ball.

near post   The goalpost closest to the player who has the ball.

nutmeg   Advancing past an opposing player by kicking the ball through that player's legs.

obstruction   Blocking an opponent's path to the ball, thereby illegally stopping him from playing the ball.

offside   A foul that's called when a player is in his opponents' half of the field, has fewer than two opponents between him and the goal, and is directly involved in the play when a teammate plays the ball.

outswinger   A ball that bends out and away from the goal.

overlapping   An attacking technique in which a defender with the ball advances past the midfield area.

penalty kick   A direct free kick, taken from the penalty spot, as a punishment for a personal foul against an attacker within the penalty area.

penalty spot The spot twelve yards in front of the goal.

push pass This kind of pass is made with the inside of the foot and usually just moves the ball a short distance.

red card The referee holds this up to indicate that a player is being ejected from the game.

return pass When the ball is passed directly back to the player who just turned it over.

running off the ball Moving without the ball, either as a decoy or to get into a position to take a pass or provide support.

save When the goalkeeper prevents the opponents from scoring a goal by catching or deflecting the ball.

screening Keeping yourself positioned between a defender and the ball or preventing a tackle or other attempt to take the ball away. Also called shielding.

small-sided This game has far fewer than eleven players on a field that's smaller than regulation.

standoff In defense, keeping goalside of an attacker, refusing to be tempted to tackle, and keeping him contained.

striker A forward whose role is to score or to be the target man.

support In offense, running near a teammate with the ball so he or she can pass it to you if necessary. In defense, staying near a tackling teammate, covering his mark if necessary.

sweeper An extra defender without his or her own mark, who might target an attacking opponent or go after stray balls.

tackling Taking the ball from your opponent.

target man This player's role is to receive long, often high passes and pass them quickly—often via a header—to a teammate.

through ball A pass that goes behind the defense where an intended receiver can run into it.

throw-in When one team sends the ball over the touchline, a player from the other team stands out, uses a two-handed throw, and releases the ball while it's over his or her head.

touchline The sideline.

trapping Getting the ball under control with any body part except the arms or hands.

volley Kicking a ball that's in midair.

wall A line of teammates positioned ten yards in front of the ball to block a free kick from the goal.

wall pass A pass that's returned back to the player who just delivered it.

winger An attacker, usually operating near the touchline.

World Cup The world championship of soccer, held every four years.

yellow card The referee holds this card up as an official warning against further misconduct by a specific player. The next step is a red card, ejection.

Ordering *Sports Rules in Pictures* is easy and convenient. Just call 1-800-631-8571 or send your order to:

The Putnam Publishing Group
390 Murray Hill Parkway, Dept. B
East Rutherford, NJ 07073
Also available at your local bookstore or wherever paperbacks are sold.

			US	CANADA
_____	Baseball Rules in Pictures	399-51597	$7.95	$10.50
_____	Official Little League Baseball Rules in Pictures	399-51531	$7.95	$10.50
_____	Softball Rules in Pictures	399-51356	$6.95	$ 9.25
_____	Football Rules in Pictures	399-51479	$7.95	$10.50
_____	Basketball Rules in Pictures	399-51590	$7.95	$10.50
_____	Hockey Rules in Pictures	399-51480	$7.95	$10.50
_____	Amateur Wrestling Rules in Pictures	399-51589	$7.95	$10.50
_____	Volleyball Rules in Pictures	399-51537	$7.95	$10.50
_____	Golf Rules in Pictures	399-51438	$7.95	$10.50
_____	Tennis Rules and Techniques in Pictures	399-51674	$7.95	$10.50
_____	Track and Field Rules in Pictures	399-51620	$7.95	$10.50
_____	Gymnastics Rules in Pictures	399-51636	$7.95	$10.50
_____	Soccer Rules in Pictures	399-51647	$7.95	$10.50
_____	Golf Techniques in Pictures	399-51664	$7.95	$10.50
_____	Soccer Techniques in Pictures	399-51701	$7.95	$10.50

Subtotal $ _____
*Postage & Handling $ _____
Sales Tax $ _____
(CA, NJ, NY, PA)
Total Amount Due $ _____
Payable in U.S. Funds
(No cash orders accepted)

*Postage & Handling: $1.00 for 1 book, $.25 for each additional book up to a maximum of $3.50.

Please send me the titles checked above. Enclosed is my:

☐ check   ☐ money order

Please charge my:

☐ Visa   ☐ MasterCard   ☐ American Express

Card # _____   Expiration date _____

Signature as on charge card _____

Name _____

Address _____

City _____   State _____   Zip _____

Please allow six weeks for delivery. Prices subject to change without notice.